BALLET P

UNIVERSITY PRESS OF FLORIDA

Florida A&M University, Tallahassee
Florida Atlantic University, Boca Raton
Florida Gulf Coast University, Ft. Myers
Florida International University, Miami
Florida State University, Tallahassee
New College of Florida, Sarasota
University of Central Florida, Orlando
University of Florida, Gainesville
University of North Florida, Jacksonville
University of South Florida, Tampa
University of West Florida, Pensacola

University Press of Florida

*Gainesville · Tallahassee · Tampa · Boca Raton
Pensacola · Orlando · Miami · Jacksonville · Ft. Myers · Sarasota*

BALLET PEDAGOGY

The Art of Teaching

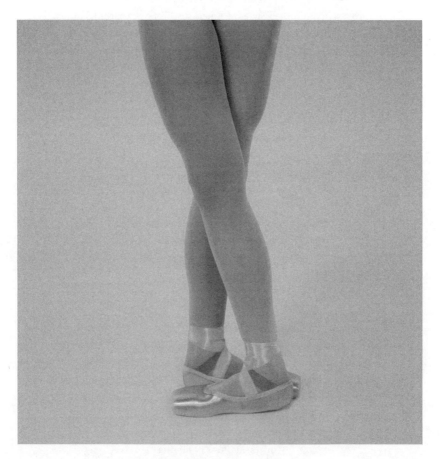

Rory Foster

Foreword by David Howard

Library of Congress Cataloging-in-Publication Data
Foster, Rory.
Ballet pedagogy: the art of teaching/Rory Foster;
foreword by David Howard.
p. cm.
Includes bibliographical references and index.
ISBN 978-0-8130-3459-1 (alk. paper)
1. Ballet—Study and teaching. I. Title.
GV1788.2.P37F67 2010
792.8079–dc22   2009041772

The University Press of Florida is the scholarly publishing agency for the
State University System of Florida, comprising Florida A&M University,
Florida Atlantic University, Florida Gulf Coast University, Florida
International University, Florida State University, New College of Florida,
University of Central Florida, University of Florida, University of North
Florida, University of South Florida, and University of West Florida.

University Press of Florida
15 Northwest 15th Street
Gainesville, FL 32611–2079
http://www.upf.com

To Kendall
with love and affection

CONTENTS

ILLUSTRATIONS

FOREWORD

Globalization has opened borders, innovations, thoughts, and creativity. This inspirational and fluid exchange of information has also occurred in our art form of dance, and it is very inspiring that Rory Foster has devoted the time and patience to comprehensively write about the art of classical ballet. Rory's background is rich and diverse. Having studied with a wide range of teachers representing different training methods, traditions, and styles, Rory presents a unique perspective and an original concept of ballet pedagogy.

It is lovely to see a former dancer having used the experiences of his performing career to develop into an excellent teacher. In this book, Rory has passed on every aspect of the knowledge required for a successful career in the teaching field.

Ballet Pedagogy contains valuable and necessary information, including teaching skills, development of a ballet class, anatomy and music for dancers, learning processes, health and injuries, and how to establish a dance school. This book is a must read for every teacher, students aspiring to teach, parents, and dancers on their way to a career. It gives straightforward information on what the dance field is like today.

David Howard
International
Master
Teacher

PREFACE

Throughout my performing and teaching career, I have watched many well-trained dancers, including seasoned professional performers, teach their first ballet class or series of classes. Many of them did not know with any certainty how to construct and sequence the barre and center floor exercises correctly for the stated age range and level of advancement, how to appropriately demonstrate and explain the proper execution of a step, smoothly deliver and pace the class, clearly articulate general and individual corrections, or how to choose the appropriate meter and rhythm or set a conducive tempo for an exercise.

This begs the question: How can well-trained dancers not know how to teach ballet class? After all, they take class daily year after year, and they repeat the same or a similar sequence of exercises at the barre and in their center floor work. Logic would suggest that constructing and sequencing a class should be second nature. The classical ballet terms are in French, yet some teachers while having danced themselves following the French directives of their teachers neglect to use French terms in their own teaching.

This conundrum is understandable if one thinks about the mind-set of aspiring students or professional dancers. They come to class focused entirely on their work, striving daily for that elusive perfection in technique and artistry. There is no time, desire, or need for that matter to be pedagogically mindful of the structure of the class or to analyze the teaching skills of the instructor. The effectiveness of the teacher is expected. The dancers are there to absorb everything they can from that class as a whole and from the corrections of the teacher as it specifically pertains to them individually. They are wholly committed to the task of perfecting their own dancing. They are not at all focused on any pedagogical skills. When the time eventually comes for them to teach, most are unprepared. They don't know what to give at particular levels (children and adults, beginning through advanced) or how to present the material. So they "wing it" and hope to learn through trial and error. Others look to someone to guide and train them in the skills of teaching.

When professional dancers begin the transition from performing to teaching and find themselves either completely lost or, at best, lacking in many of the essential pedagogical skills and knowledge, they also have to confront and clear the psychological transition hurdle from that of self-focused dancer to that of teacher, the constant giver who is simultaneously focused on many individuals.

Gifted teachers, just like great choreographers and dancers, have certain intrinsic "sparks" that take them to the higher levels of creativity and accomplishment in their art. They must have the innate ability to demonstrate precisely, understand the role and importance of music, identify errors, and articulate corrections in easily understandable ways for each student at every level. But even without these inherent attributes, the ability to train and develop into a fine teacher can be accomplished through a strong desire and commitment and by honing and refining one's teaching skills and techniques.

I was inspired to write this book after many years of teaching undergraduate and graduate pedagogy courses to ballet and modern dance majors. I have methodically defined and analyzed all of the pedagogical elements that pertain to the planning and teaching of a ballet class. Although these elements address the art and skill of teaching classical ballet, nearly every pedagogical component here can be applied to modern dance or any form of concert dance.

I have addressed what I feel are important reinforcements to the novice teacher, specifically, essential components regarding execution of technique and common errors, the structural development of the foot and its use in pointe work, understanding correct anatomical placement, balance and counterbalance, and how to work with music along with live and recorded accompaniment.

Other chapters cover dance-related injuries, approaches to structuring classes and how to notate them, planning out your technique curriculum according to your goals and objectives over a designated period, presenting and teaching the class, and establishing your own school. The significant chapter on teaching delivery includes the elements of explanation and demonstration, pacing, vocal presentation and teaching demeanor, establishing and maintaining an effective level of energy, correcting your students using touch and imagery, and being effective with music. Additionally, I give some insight into the learning process and the teacher/student relationship, as well as what a new teacher can expect.

Understanding the historical development of ballet technique and training is important for all teachers to know, so I begin with a synopsis of the evolution of the *danse d'ecole* and the establishment of some of the major schools or systems of ballet training.

There are distinctions between teaching a children's class (ages 8–11) and older students, and I address these when it is appropriate. However, it is not my intention in this book to dictate any sort of syllabus for various graded levels of classes, nor to explain in any detail the technicalities of how to execute barre and center floor exercises. Excellent books have been written on these subjects.

The contents of this book are based on the presumption that anyone who is setting out to teach classical ballet has had years of studio training from a knowledgeable and competent teacher and, therefore, has a thorough theoretical and practical understanding of how to execute all of the barre exercises and center floor work at least through an intermediate level, along with rudimentary pointe work.

I have tried to make the material comprehensive enough for the experienced teacher, yet simplistic enough for the novice. Although this book can be used as a reference for experienced teachers who are analyzing and self-critiquing their own classes and teaching skills, I have written it principally for those who are starting their teaching career—both the student teacher and the transitioning professional dancer. It is a teaching manual to guide and help them formulate, construct, and teach a ballet class.

ACKNOWLEDGMENTS

I wish to express my sincere gratitude to everyone who encouraged me and gave me assistance during the realization of this book. I wish to thank all of my teachers for imparting a wealth of knowledge to me throughout my career and American Ballet Theatre for giving me the opportunity to work in my art alongside many of our greatest dancers and choreographers.

I shall always be indebted to David Howard for all that he taught me as a dancer and teacher and for taking the time to review my manuscript and prepare the foreword. I wish to express my appreciation to Dina Makarova for her beautiful cover photograph of Natalia Makarova and Ivan Nagy. I also wish to thank Kristen Wenrick and Walt Strange for the use of the Louisville Academy of Dance studios and Natalia Ashikhmina of the Louisville Ballet and Katherine Sawicki for demonstrating the studio ballet positions.

Finally, I wish to thank Kendall DuVay for her encouragement, unwavering support, and overall assistance in the final preparation of this book.

Introduction

I have been fortunate in my career to have had excellent training, studying under many world-renowned teachers such as David Howard, Vincenzo Celli (Cecchetti Method), Valentina Pereyaslavec and Vera Volkova (Vaganova), Benjamin Harkarvy, Harold Christiansen, Maria Fey, and many teachers from the Sadler's Wells/Royal Ballet who passed down the combined Franco-Russian and Italian techniques of the Imperial Russian Ballet. Over time and especially when I began to teach, I realized that the effectiveness of any one school or training system does not lie intrinsically in the curriculum or syllabus. It is the teacher's art and skill of imparting that knowledge and the ability to solve technical and artistic errors in his/her students that bring the training process to a level of success.

I began teaching professional dancers and young students when I was the company ballet master for the New Orleans Ballet and Chicago Ballet and a teacher in their professional schools. Eventually, I moved into higher education, teaching in conservatory-based university programs.

I also teach nationally and internationally in arts academies and conservatories, professional ballet and modern dance companies, and private studios. This has enabled me over the years to see how students are trained, coming from so many diverse schools, systems, and methodologies. I have observed throughout the country many wonderful teachers and enormously talented and gifted students who have extraordinary facility and physiques and the potential to develop into superb artists with successful careers in ballet and concert dance companies.

Conversely, I continue to see many students with training discrepancies and technical problems, as well as poorly qualified teachers whose teaching constitutes a disservice to their students. The following points are flaws that

I observe generally in the training progression of dancers and the manner in which teachers instruct.

Ballet students must be taught in a manner that gives them a greater understanding of how their bodies move and why they do what they are doing. Each ballet exercise in all of the prominent training methods is designed for a specific purpose in their training. This was a key component behind Agrippina Vaganova's theory of training when she developed her system.

Many students, including ones at advanced levels, lack a thorough understanding of technique and how the body must move as a coordinated whole. The connection between the torso and the legs often does not work in sync—moving in an integrated, harmonized, and graceful way. Students do not move from their center—the solar plexus. They go into positions where they look posed and static, like mannequins—the head being cocked at a prescribed angle with the eyes glued to the outstretched arm or hand, or they just stare out into space, devoid of any imagery or feeling for how their *épaulement* and upper body contribute to the entire shape and the dynamic breadth of the position or how the directed focus of the eyes finishes off the completion of the classical line. They grip their muscles in order to hold their placement, and as a result their positions don't look alive. The essential dynamic quality is lost.

Proper use of the *plié* is not stressed. The *plié* is what a dancer moves through in order to get into the next step or directional change. It propels the dancer up into the jump, and it supports the subsequent landing. *Plié* is the most essential movement in dance; it is not a static position. Weight transference, changes of direction and levels, plus transition and connecting steps require its continuous and correct use. Students often go too deeply—stopping the energetic dynamics of a step—or they resist the natural flow of the *plié* and make it too shallow.

Too little attention is paid to the importance of connecting steps such as *glissade, pas de bourrée, soutenu, balancé,* etc., which link primary steps. Connecting steps must be danced with the same purity and accuracy as primary steps. Also, students don't pay attention to, or are not taught, the rhythmical dynamics of connecting steps, along with the full articulation of their feet, use of the floor, and the accuracy of the five positions. The incorporation of musicality—timing and accent—is sorely deficient.

Much more attention needs to be given to the articulation and strength of the feet. Too often they look lazy. Using the resistance of the floor when the foot is required to brush in and out during certain barre exercises and allegro steps will make the foot strong and supple.

Incorrect posture and placement and the incorrect use of turnout compound the technical problems. Students do not maintain their center axis of balance and often sit back on their supporting heel—locking back into their knee—or they have their weight pitched too far over their toes, which when standing on one leg causes them to sit into the supporting hip and puts undue strain on their knee and ankle tendons, especially when performing a *fondu*.

Turnout (rotation) of the working leg is sacrificed for an absolute 90° direction in *á la seconde*, or worse, working the leg behind second position. As a result, the heel is turned toward the back instead of rotated forward, and when the leg is lifted *en l'air*, the pelvis is wrongly displaced, throwing off the body's center alignment and counterbalance.

A primary training goal of all teachers is to insist that their students dance with an unmannered simplicity of style and purity of line. All too often students in their desire to be expressive exaggerate their dancing, especially their *port de bras*, creating mannerisms that are very difficult to undo and that are not reflective of pure classical ballet.

Dance is a plastic art wherein we use our body as the instrument to create continuously changing shapes and lines. This requires focused concentration and an internal awareness—both visually and kinetically—of every part of our body as a whole. The mirror should be used only as a tool to periodically glance at and check the accuracy of movement and line, for it is the dancer's own consciousness of feeling movement and shape that is most important.

Many students do not use the mirror correctly during center floor work as a fundamental tool of their training. They have not been taught how to peripherally glimpse into the mirror. Instead, they stare—their eyes rarely leaving their reflection. They become mesmerized with themselves. As a result, they don't really see how they are performing a step in a technical and analytical way. Instead of their awareness being directed inward to the kinetic feeling of a movement, it is visually directed outward into their reflection in the mirror. **Watching** their reflection dance eclipses the **feeling** of their body in movement. Also, as their gaze, or visual focus, is stuck in the mirror, the head often does not move in coordination with the body, nor does it follow the correct shape and line of a position or step. Choreographer Agnes de Mille said, "The practice mirror is to be used for corrections of faults, not for a love affair, and the figure you watch should not become your dearest friend."

In my early years of training with my teachers from the Royal Ballet, class was never taught with the dancers facing a mirror. The mirrors were placed on the side wall. In Maestro Celli's New York studio, dancers took class with their backs to the mirror. The principle behind this is that the teacher's discerning eye acts in place of the mirror for the student. When the actual mirror is needed and used properly, it functions not as a narcissistic medium but simply as a tool which helps the student see (by the visual learning process) and apply the teacher's corrections and modifications. Once a dancer reaches the advanced/professional level, it is more acceptable to work in front of a mirrored wall because by that time those dancers know how to use the mirror correctly as a tool.

Finally, one of the most obvious examples of not seeing what students should see and feel is the incorrect line and direction of positions when they square off and direct their focus to the corners of the room instead of the points of their own personal square. Ballet, along with all concert dance, is a proscenium art form and thus is choreographed and performed with the front—the audience—as the constant reference point for line and direction. Dancers must learn to use space in relation to the front (audience) along with the eight points of direction within their own square.

These observations of training deficiencies can be seen everywhere to some degree, and they are the result of lackadaisical learning and/or poor teaching skills. It is our teaching responsibility to inspire and train aspiring students so they may develop strength, flexibility, a clean and precise technique, and the ability to move with aplomb, musically and artistically.

The pedagogical skills that I cover in this book are the tools we use to help us plan and deliver an effective ballet class. I do not delve deeply into the "correct way" to teach technique, as this will certainly cause disagreement between those who come from different training backgrounds. In this area concerning technique, I touch upon only those points which I believe are universally acknowledged by well-trained teachers from all methods.

But before addressing the art of ballet pedagogy, having some historical knowledge of the development of our art form and its training methods is a good starting point for all teachers, especially those who have not studied ballet history. So we begin with a historical synopsis of the *danse d'école*.

On with the dance!

1

Danse d'École

A HISTORICAL SYNOPSIS
OF BALLET PEDAGOGY

Most ballet careers are short-lived. And when dancers retire, they quickly become unknown to newer generations of aspiring ballet dancers. Ask most students today if they know anything about—or have even heard of— Sergei Diaghilev, Ninette de Valois, Margot Fonteyn, Antony Tudor, Igor Youskevitch, Lucia Chase, or Erik Bruhn, and the answer will usually be no. They only know those dancers who are on the current roster of companies and those they read about in current periodicals like *Pointe* and *Dance Magazine*. The history, tradition, and evolution of ballet performance and training are not part of the dance curriculum in most schools.

Danse d'école is the French term for classical theatrical dancing (ballet). The following is a brief historical and chronological synopsis of the *danse d'école* and some of the more important people and icons who were responsible for its growth and refinement. It is knowledge of our artistic heritage which all teachers of classical ballet should know.

The beginnings of court dance where steps were first referred to as ballet can be traced back to the lavish festivities given in the courts of Renaissance Italy by Lorenzo de Medici (1449–92), ruler of Florence and patron of the arts. In the late sixteenth century, his granddaughter, Catherine de Medici (1519–89) Queen of France, introduced to the French court great entertainment spectacles similar to those presented by her grandfather. These productions fused the art forms of dance, drama, instrumental, and vocal music, and design. The most notable was the *Ballet Comique de la Reine* (1581), which is considered to be the first ballet.

It was during the reign of Louis XIV (the Sun King, 1638–1715) that ballet enjoyed great popularity as part of the king's lavish royal presentations. Louis considered himself an accomplished dancer, often performing in the ballets that were part of his great court fêtes, and it was during his reign that ballet began to evolve as an independent art form. However, the look of ballet back then was a far cry from how we view it today: it was mostly members of the court who performed, and they did so in heavy, cumbersome ankle-length costumes, plus they wore hard, heeled shoes and covered their faces with leather masks. This was not very comfortable or conducive to any sort of intricate or technical movement. Additionally, the choreography during this period expressed and preserved the air of nobility as was reflected through the etiquette and traditions of the royal court. This was known as *ballet de cour.*

The nascent art of ballet found fertile ground in France. Pierre Beauchamp (1636–1705) was the dancing master to Louis XIV and appeared in many ballets with the king. He is credited with naming the five positions of ballet, around 1700, and establishing technique through the use of turnout and the virtuosity of turns and jumps. Beauchamp broke away from the restrictive formal court style of *ballet de cour* and formulated the technical system of classical dance known as *danse d'école*. Historically, it is here that the technical nuances of classic ballet as we know it commenced. Through Louis XIV, the Royal Academy of Music and Dance was founded with Beauchamp as its ballet master. Today it is known as the Paris Opéra.

The next great figure of the *danse d'école* was Jean-Georges Noverre (1727–1810). He is known as the "Grandfather of the Ballet." Noverre was a renowned choreographer and ballet master who worked in the great opera houses of Europe. He was eventually appointed ballet master of the Paris Opéra, a post he held until the French Revolution in 1789. Noverre further reformed ballet from the limited, restrictive and conventionalized presentation of movement into a truly dynamic art form, introducing the *ballet d'action*. He is responsible for laying down many of the principles that govern ballet today. In 1760, he published his famous *Lettres sur la danse et sur les ballets,* which set forth his ideas regarding ballet as an artistic medium.

In *Let's Meet the Ballet,* Dorothy Samachson writes, "Noverre introduced the *pas d'action*, the step of action, of pantomime used to advance the story of the ballet. This and other innovations helped break the rigid formula of court dances, and led to the development of the dramatic possibilities of the ballet. . . . Noverre also championed reform in costumes, and he showed that musician, choreographer, and designer must work together in creating a ballet."

Noverre's creative and pedagogical gifts resulted in a great heritage of outstanding performers and teachers, most notably Auguste Vestris (1760–1842). With his soaring elevation and dazzling virtuosity he became a premier danseur at the Paris Opéra, one of Europe's greatest dancers, and was dubbed *le dieu de la danse* (the god of dance). Vestris later opened his own school in Paris, and many of his pupils carried on the tradition of the *danse d'école* and Noverre's principles, including August Bournonville, Charles Didelot, Jules Perrot, Marius Petipa, and Marie Taglioni.

Until the French Revolution, Paris was the center of dance in Europe. Ballet was not entirely dominated by French artists, however. Dancers, teachers, and choreographers from throughout Europe were drawn to France. After the Revolution, many artists of the ballet community fled to teach and perform in safer capitals and cultural centers. Paris and its French School, which gave the art of ballet the graceful movement of *adagio*, was no longer the leader of European dance.

The Italian School, with its improved technique and dynamic turns and elevation, thus rose in prominence. The Italian technique gave us the movement of *allegro*. Beginning with the choreographer and teacher Carlo Blasis (1795–1878), immense progress was made in the codification of the vocabulary of ballet and a more structured training methodology. Blasis was of the direct lineage of Noverre, having studied with Salvatore Vigano, who studied under Noverre's protégé, Jean Dauberval.

In his *Lettres sur la danse*, Noverre instructed us on *what* ballet should be. Blasis taught us *how* to do it; he codified classical ballet technique. Blasis published *An Elementary Treatise upon the Theory and Practice of the Art of Dancing* (1820) and *The Code of Terpsichore* (1830). They were the first comprehensive books on ballet technique as we understand it today. Blasis explained the construction of the ballet class, called "the lesson," which consists of barre work, *adagio, pirouettes, allegro,* etc., and remains the founda-

Fig. 1.1. *Attitude croisé devant.*

tion of every dancer's daily training to the present day. He introduced the "attitude" position and also established the technique of spotting when doing multiple turns to avoid getting dizzy. Every dancer knows the canon of spotting: "The head is the last to leave and the first to get there."

In 1837, Blasis was made director of the Imperial Ballet Academy, which was associated with the Royal Opera House (La Scala) in Milan. Under his

Fig. 1.2. *Attitude effacé derrière.*

leadership, it became the most prestigious classical ballet academy in the world. Blasis trained most of the great Italian dancers and teachers of that time, including Giovanni Lepri, who was the teacher of Enrico Cecchetti. *The Code of Terpsichore* eventually became the standard of instruction as teachers from the Imperial Academy traveled all over Europe and Russia spreading Blasis's fundamentals and the Italian technique.

Ballet in Russia

Ballet in Russia was initially dominated by the French technique. The French School of ballet embodied a cultivated soft and graceful style of movement. It did not have the powerful and energetic virtuosity exemplified by the Italians. The French and Italian styles of ballet technique and training would eventually come together to form the great Russian technique.

In 1738 in St. Petersburg, by imperial decree of the empress Anna, the first Russian school of theatrical dance was founded. It was the initiative of the French ballet master and teacher Jean-Baptiste Landé. It was later to be known as the Imperial Theatre School.

Charles-Louis Didelot (1767–1837), who studied under Noverre, Jean Dauberval, and Auguste Vestris, was appointed ballet master of the Imperial Russian Ballet and Imperial Theatre School in 1801, and he set into motion the first great period of Russian ballet. Didelot produced many ballets, and through the reorganization of the Imperial Theatre School, he raised the level of ballet training to a higher standard. He is considered the "father of the Russian ballet."

The Imperial Russian Ballet was the resident company of the Imperial Theatre in St. Petersburg (also known as the Bolshoi Theatre). It also gave performances at the Maryinsky Theatre during the 1880s and in 1889 moved from the Imperial Theatre to the Maryinsky. It was known as the Maryinsky Ballet up until the Russian Revolution. The Imperial Theatre School remained the official school of the Imperial Russian Ballet.

Christian Johansson (1817–1903) made his debut with the Imperial Russian Ballet in 1841 as partner to Marie Taglioni. Johansson was a student of August Bournonville, the great icon of the Royal Danish Ballet and himself a product of French training and the ideals and tradition of Noverre through his teacher, Auguste Vestris. As the stature of the male dancer declined in Europe during the Romantic era, and the women of the ballet reigned supreme, Johansson did much to maintain the importance of men in the Imperial Russian Ballet, thus keeping ballet strong and viable in Russia.

Johansson remained in Russia as a leading dancer and became one of the most influential teachers in the Imperial School. He refined the training, creating a greater purity of technique, which established a new standard for the Russian classical style.

The Italian Influence

The Imperial Maryinsky Ballet engaged the famous Italian dancer Virginia Zucchi as guest ballerina from 1885 until 1892. A pupil of Blasis and a brilliant technician with extraordinary artistic qualities, Zucchi was the first to bring to Russia the forceful virtuosity of the Italian technique. She was the catalyst that drove the Imperial School to adopt a more rigorous methodology of training as typified in her dancing.

The virtuosity of the Italian dancers with their dazzling turns and soaring elevation amazed the audiences. With their strong and brilliant technique, the Italians rose to dominance in the Imperial School. This is not to say, however, that the French tradition of technique was totally eclipsed. With the introduction of the great Italian ballet master Enrico Cecchetti's method of instruction combined with the heritage of Johansson's Franco-Russian technique and style, the Imperial Ballet produced some of the greatest dancers in history: Vaslav Nijinsky, Anna Pavlova, Nicholas Legat, Tamara Karsavina, Olga Preobrajenska and Olga Spessivtzeva.

Enrico Cecchetti (1850–1928) made his debut with the Imperial Russian Ballet at the Maryinsky Theatre in 1887. He worked under Marius Petipa, the French choreographer who created some of our greatest classical ballets: *Don Quixote, La Bayadère, The Sleeping Beauty, Raymonda,* and *The Seasons.* Cecchetti had an excellent technique and gift for doing mime. He performed the virtuoso role of the Blue Bird as well as the mime role of Carabosse in the premiere of Petipa's *The Sleeping Beauty* in 1890. He became second ballet master to the Maryinsky Ballet and began teaching at the Imperial School. When Sergei Diaghilev formed the Ballets Russes, many of his principal dancers who were from the Maryinsky did not want to leave St. Petersburg on performance tours because they would have to forgo their daily ballet class with Maestro Cecchetti. So in 1909, Diaghilev offered Cecchetti the position of company ballet master, which he accepted.

Cecchetti was one of the greatest ballet teachers in history. He developed a teaching method that expanded upon the principles of Blasis. Cecchetti studied under Giovanni Lepri, a pupil of Blasis. The method he developed is unique: each day of the week there are comprehensive set combinations of exercises to be performed, which run the gamut of the classical ballet vocabulary. Dance historian Cyril Beaumont wrote, "What impressed me most about the Cecchetti method of teaching was the way in which each exercise played a definite and planned part in the student's technical development. There is nothing haphazard about the system, nothing which depended on the teacher's mood of the moment. There is a definite plan to daily classes."

Cecchetti later opened a school in London, and around 1918 he systematically set down his method for training dancers. In 1922, Beaumont published *A Manual of the Theory and Practice of Classical Theatrical Dancing (Méthod Cecchetti)*. Beaumont and Cecchetti along with a few of his students founded the Cecchetti Society in 1922 for the purpose of preserving and protecting his methodology. Charter members included Cecchetti's protégé, Margaret Craske, Marie Rambert (founding director of Ballet Rambert), and Ninette de Valois (founding director of the Royal Ballet). Branches of the Society have continued to be active in many countries, and Cecchetti's method is still widely taught throughout the world.

Ballet in the Soviet Union

There was great uncertainty, for a time, regarding the future of the Maryinsky Ballet after the Russian Revolution of 1917 and the two years of civil war that followed. The performing arts, like every other aspect of Russian life, were controlled by the revolutionary Soviet bureaucracy. But, fortunately, the ballet flourished under the new order of the Soviet Union. And the emerging Soviet ballet had a fresh, energetic, and acrobatic style in its technique and presentation. The Maryinsky became the Kirov Ballet. St. Petersburg became Leningrad. And a retired ballerina by the name of Agrippina Vaganova (1789–1951) established a new era in ballet pedagogy.

Vaganova was trained at the Imperial Ballet School under luminary teachers: Legat, Vazem, and Ivanov. She joined the Maryinsky Ballet in 1897 and was promoted to a principal ballerina in 1915. Vaganova was known as the "queen of variations," renowned for her jumps and *batterie*. In 1921 she became a teacher at the Leningrad State Ballet School, the former Imperial Ballet School of St. Petersburg.

Soviet critics of the new Leningrad State School of the Kirov Ballet were of the opinion that the school was too conservative and backward and that it lacked creativity. They demanded reform. It was during this period that Vaganova strived to find a more effective means of training classical dancers. She developed and tested a technique and method of instruction during the 1920s that she based on the fluid, expressive, and graceful plasticity of the French School and the bravura virtuosity of the Italian style. She also incorporated the aspects of the more forceful and acrobatic Soviet ballet that developed after the Revolution. Vaganova became the greatest Russian teacher of her day, and her system of training continues to be taught at the Vaganova Choreographic Institute at the Kirov Ballet in St. Petersburg and throughout the world. World-renowned dancers such as Natalia Makarova, Rudolph Nureyev, and Mikhail Baryshnikov trained under the Vaganova system.

The Royal Academy of Dancing

The high standards of training in the French, Russian, and Italian methods were maintained by state-supported institutions such as the Paris Opera, Kirov, and La Scala. Their schools had formal curricula for each level of training, and there was consistency in the manner in which ballet technique was taught. No such institution existed in Britain in 1920, and the quality of training in most schools was poor. A distinguished group of resident exponents of these training methods met for the purpose of raising the quality and consistency of ballet training: Eduardo Espinosa, French; Tamara Karsavina, Russian; Lucia Cormani, Italian; and Phyllis Bedells, English. They formed the Association of Operatic Dancing of Great Britain and developed examinations syllabi for all member teachers to follow. King George V granted a royal charter to the Association in 1936, and it was renamed the Royal Academy of Dancing (RAD).

The RAD system of training has graded syllabi from elementary to advanced levels along with studies that combine performance, choreography, anatomy, dance notation, dance appreciation, and other related areas. The RAD syllabus is taught by certified RAD instructors all over the world.

The Cecchetti, RAD, and Vaganova systems are the most influential and widely known methods of classical ballet training in the world today. In addition to these, it is important to acknowledge the Bournonville technique from a historical reference point and the Balanchine style, which is influencing many major schools, particularly in the United States.

Bournonville

August Bournonville (1805–1879) was a Danish dancer, choreographer, and teacher. He studied in Copenhagen with his father, Antoine, and in Paris with Auguste Vestris. He danced with the Paris Opéra and with the Royal Danish Ballet. In 1848, he gave up performing and devoted himself entirely to teaching and choreography, creating more than 61 ballets. He was strongly influenced by the French School, but he created a style that was uniquely his own. It was distinctively Romantic and had superior technical precision. These qualities are reflected in his *Fifty Enchaînements* (classroom combinations of exercises), which make up the foundation of the Bournonville technique. It is still taught to this day as a separate class within the overall training curriculum in the school of the Royal Danish Ballet. According to Anatole Chujoy and P. W. Manchester, in their *Dance Encyclopedia*, "It is to Bournonville that the Royal Danish Ballet owes its particular character and unique style, which is the only surviving link with the ballet of the mid-nineteenth century before the Russian dominance began toward the end of the century."

Balanchine

George Balanchine (1904–83) received his training at the Imperial Ballet School, which, by the time he graduated in 1921, had been renamed the Leningrad State Ballet School. He began choreographing when he was a teenager, and by the time he was 20, he had become the fifth and last choreographer for Diaghilev's Ballets Russes. Balanchine was strongly influenced by the classicism of Marius Petipa and by Michael Fokine's *Les Sylphides*, which reflected Fokine's revolutionary Five Principles. He choreographed for ballet companies as well as for Broadway shows, motion pictures, and even for the circus. He was one of the most prolific choreographers in the history of ballet.

Balanchine came to America in 1934 at the invitation of Lincoln Kirstein, who wished to form a ballet company. Mr. B uttered the now famous words, "But first, a school," and so together they founded the School of American Ballet (SAB) in New York City. In 1946 they formed the Ballet Society, which became the New York City Ballet (NYCB) in 1948 and the resident company of the City Center of Music and Drama.

SAB is linked to the tradition of the Maryinsky Ballet through Balanchine and other dancers who followed him to America, most notably Alexandra Danilova. Over time, SAB developed its own teaching methodology and began producing most of the dancers entering NYCB.

Over the decades, Balanchine's choreographic style and his particular use of movement dynamics developed into a new and distinctive way to dance. Lightness, precision footwork, and amazing speed are the dominant qualities in the execution of his choreography. He also took the traditional classic line and gave it a more angular plasticity.

Balanchine's style of choreography spread throughout the world as more and more companies added his ballets to their repertoire. His work influenced a multitude of new choreographers, and many have emulated the Balanchine look. SAB evolved its teaching methodology incorporating this stylistic look and approach to placement and technique; it reflects Balanchine's interpretations of classical ballet technique and trains dancers to move with the kind of speed and dynamics inherent in Balanchine's choreography. It is now officially known as the Balanchine Technique® and the Balanchine Style®.

Dancers who worked with Mr. B in NYCB and attended his daily company class have differing personal interpretations of what he conveyed in his class and rehearsals and how he wanted his dancers to move. To date, the definitive book is *Suki Schorer on Balanchine Technique*, by Suki Schorer.

American Ballet Theatre National Training Curriculum

The most recent training system is the American Ballet Theatre (ABT) National Training Curriculum, which was launched nationally in 2008. It was designed by Franco De Vita, principal of the ABT Jacqueline Kennedy Onassis School, and Raymond Lukens, artistic associate of the ABT/NYU master's degree program. It incorporates elements of the French, Italian, and Russian schools and consists of seven levels of training plus a pre-ballet primary level. Goals and objectives are set for each level, but it is up to the individual teacher to design exercises to accomplish them. What makes this curriculum unique is that it takes a more holistic approach with teachers by addressing the areas of anatomy and kinesiology, dance-related injuries—prevention and recovery—nutrition, psychology and child development, risk management, and medical and facility guidelines.

These methods, old and new, are the pedagogical systems that we currently have in classical ballet. There are many opinions regarding the strengths

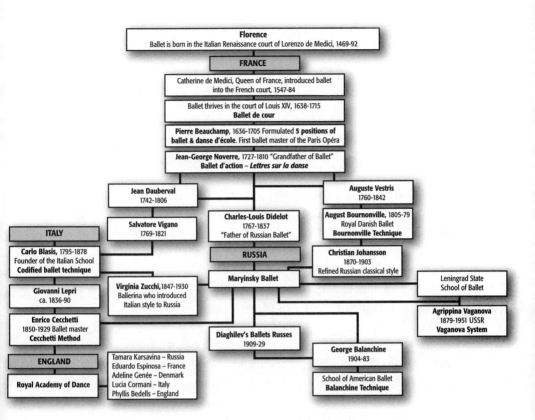

Florence
Ballet is born in the Italian Renaissance court of Lorenzo de Medici, 1469-92

FRANCE

Catherine de Medici, Queen of France, introduced ballet into the French court, 1547-84

Ballet thrives in the court of Louis XIV, 1638-1715
Ballet de cour

Pierre Beauchamp, 1636-1705 Formulated **5 positions of ballet & danse d'école**. First ballet master of the Paris Opéra

Jean-George Noverre, 1727-1810 "Grandfather of Ballet"
Ballet d'action – *Lettres sur la danse*

Jean Dauberval
1742-1806

Auguste Vestris
1760-1842

Salvatore Vigano
1769-1821

Charles-Louis Didelot
1767-1837
"Father of Russian Ballet"

August Bournonville, 1805-79
Royal Danish Ballet
Bournonville Technique

ITALY

Carlo Blasis, 1795-1878
Founder of the Italian School
Codified ballet technique

RUSSIA

Christian Johansson
1870-1903
Refined Russian classical style

Leningrad State School of Ballet

Giovanni Lepri
ca. 1836-90

Virginia Zucchi, 1847-1930
Ballerina who introduced Italian style to Russia

Maryinsky Ballet

Agrippina Vaganova
1879-1951 USSR
Vaganova System

Enrico Cecchetti
1850-1929 Ballet master
Cecchetti Method

Diaghilev's Ballets Russes
1909-29

George Balanchine
1904-83

ENGLAND

Tamara Karsavina – Russia
Eduardo Espinosa – France
Adeline Genée – Denmark
Lucia Cormani – Italy
Phyllis Bedells – England

Royal Academy of Dance

School of American Ballet
Balanchine Technique

Diagram 1.1. History of the *danse d'école*.

and weaknesses of each teaching method. Dancers and teachers are usually very loyal to their training background, thinking that their system is the best. Suffice it to say, all of these methods of training have integrity and have produced fine dancers.

The art of ballet has had an illustrious history and evolution spanning more than 300 years since Beauchamp named the five positions of ballet. And the look of ballet has radically changed since the rigid style of Louis XIV and his court. We can't really relate today's ballet dancing to those times, but we can relate to it as far back as the mid-nineteenth century, when women began to wear tutus and to dance on pointe. The Romantic ballet is the more relevant historical reference point for us, as *Giselle* and *La Sylphide* are still performed with regularity and are considered the cornerstone of any classical company's repertoire. Therefore, this synopsis would not be complete without devoting a few words to the Romantic era and how it impacted the presentation of classical ballet.

Romantic Ballet and the Introduction of Pointe Dancing

Romanticism began in Germany and England in the late 1700s, and by 1820 it had spread throughout Europe. Romantics possessed the power of imagination and lived life intuitively according to what they felt in their hearts, focusing on expressing individuality and personal sentiment and a free play of creativity and emotions—love being the most celebrated.

The Romantic movement developed through literature, painting, music, and the ballet. The Romantics revived the unseen Gothic (medieval) world of the mysterious and supernatural. The material and ethereal worlds of mortals, witches, sylphs, fairies, and willies came together through fairy tales, folk legends, and dramatic themes of love. Théophile Gautier, the great writer/poet, created the story of *Giselle*, one of the greatest of all Romantic ballets.

The essential characteristic of the Romantic ballet is the treatment of the story on two planes: Reality of the material world and the Ideal or spiritual plane, ending with bitter Reality triumphant over the beautiful dream. The stories of *Giselle* and *La Sylphide* have ethereal creatures from a supernatural plane who move with lightness and amorphous qualities.

The art of ballet was greatly transformed by Romanticism. Lighter costumes were introduced for the women, including the long tutu, which gave them freer mobility and allowed them to execute a broader range of steps. New steps enriched the classical repertoire along with greater precision, and women began to dominate the art. But what was most revolutionary was that ballerinas began to dance on pointe. This symbolized their floating ethereal nature inherent in their Romantic character and the desire for greater heights toward the Ideal and less contact with the earth, symbolizing Reality.

This illusion of weightlessness was first introduced theatrically by Charles-Louis Didelot around 1795. His flying machine used wires attached to the dancers that whisked them into the air as they rose onto their toes. But it was Marie Taglioni who is credited with introducing ballet *sur la pointe* when she danced on her toes in *La Sylphide* in Paris in 1832. She artistically conveyed the lightness and ethereal quality of her Romantic character, the Sylph. It was the first great Romantic ballet, and it ushered the whole art of ballet into a new era.

✺

The shoes that Taglioni wore were not the same type of shoe that we know today as pointe shoes. Because their shoes were made of soft satin and leather without any supportive box or reinforcement, ballerinas of that period were only able to be on their toes for limited amounts of time and could perform only the simplest types of movement, mostly on two feet, i.e., *relevés*, *piqués*, *bourrées*, etc. A flexible leather sole gave some support, but not much, and darning the ends of the shoes rendered some padded support. (Darning the tip, or platform, was a practice that was common well into the late twentieth century.)

As ballet technique developed and became more refined and exact through Carlo Blasis's teaching and the Italian School, more and more virtuoso dancing was done on pointe, including multiple turns and longer balances. This necessitated better shoes, which Italian shoemakers began to design and produce, most notably Nicolini. Pointe shoes continued to evolve as the Italian technique made its impact on Russian ballet and on into the twentieth century with Diaghilev's Ballets Russes.

Today there are pointe shoes designed for every anatomical type of foot, including many abnormalities. Finding and choosing the most comfortable and correct shoe can be daunting. Shoes vary by length and width, qualities of shanks, types of outer and inner soles, design of the box, length of vamps, shape of the platform, etc. We have certainly come a long way since Taglioni first went up on pointe.

For teachers who need a reference guide for finding the best pointe shoes for their students, *The Pointe Book*, by Janice Barringer and Sarah Schlesinger, is an excellent resource.

2

The Ballet Class

Identifying Goals and Developing Your Objectives

When it comes to the technical and artistic execution of a step, dancers are not reticent about voicing an opinion as to the **correct** way to do it. They can be quite opinionated, even myopic, and at times critical of other schools that vary in approach from their own tradition of training. Dancers, universally, are passionately loyal to their ballet pedigree, and so they will sometimes portray a dogmatic attitude of superiority for their training heritage. I am of the opinion that this attitude has more to do with their level of knowledge and comfort in the school in which they feel most familiar, along with a deep sense of loyalty and respect for their teachers. Most dancers that I know hold their teachers, especially the early ones, in high esteem.

There are multiple approaches to teaching ballet according to traditional methods or schools. Each method follows a sequentially progressive syllabus for each year or level of instruction that addresses the training goals and objectives from which barre and center exercises are constructed and taught.

It is difficult at times to know what it means when a teacher or school claims to instruct in one of the established methods, such as Vaganova or Cecchetti. Does it mean that the complete seven- or eight-year curriculum is taught? Or does the instruction only follow the principles underlying the method? Perhaps it is simply the arm and basic body positions, *épaulement,* and *arabesques* of the method. Has the teacher actually trained to be an instructor in the method s/he claims to teach, or is s/he just teaching what s/he was taught by his/her own teacher?

Agrippina Vaganova's system is an eight-year curriculum based on her training principles, which can be found in her book, *Basic Principles of Classical Ballet: Russian Ballet Technique*, which many teachers around the world follow. Her protégé, Vera Kostrovitskaya, describes each of the lessons for each year of the Vaganova system in her book, *100 Lessons in Classical Ballet*. Likewise, the Cecchetti Method has its principles, specific exercises, and set examinations. While some methods consist of a complete training curriculum with fixed sets of daily lessons along with examinations for each year of study, others do not. The Royal Academy of Dancing (RAD) syllabus is not considered a training curriculum. RAD-trained teachers are taught to develop their own lesson plans for each level based on the examination syllabus. The RAD syllabus is intended to be used only for examination purposes (even though many teachers use it as a lesson plan). The ABT National Training Curriculum (NTC) also follows a progressive syllabus for each year of instruction. As in RAD, NTC teachers are responsible for developing the exercises that correspond to the vocabulary of movements within the training objectives of each level.

Some teachers in America have completed teacher training in RAD, Cecchetti, etc., but most have not. American ballet training is typically taught by teachers who have an eclectic training pedigree and do not follow one of the established ballet curricula. I know of very few teachers, including retired professional dancers from major companies, who have formally trained to be teachers. Most start out by simply going into the studio and teaching as best they can.

There are some teachers who assume that all they need to know to be successful and effective are the contents of the syllabus, which will either include methodical exercises and combinations or a guideline of ballet vocabulary. It is important to recognize that all of the training methods/systems in ballet are simply tools—specific approaches to the teaching process. The efficacy and successful outcome of a student's training lie in the teacher's ability and effectiveness in using this tool. Knowing how to use this tool effectively requires good teaching skills. These do not come automatically through learning and memorizing a particular syllabus, nor do methodologies inherently delineate skills such as proper demonstration, counting, correcting, musicality, anatomical approach, et cetera. These skills are taught in formal training sessions, or they are learned through experience.

Teachers fulfill the goals and objectives of a teaching method by successfully constructing, demonstrating, and explaining how to dance each step and exercise. Some teachers have great difficulty accomplishing this task. There are many who give very few, if any, individual or general corrections—they simply **give** class rather than **teach** class. What I mean by this is that they do not fully break down and explain the technique, anatomical alignment, and musicality of steps and how they connect within an exercise, nor do they inspire their students to dance a combination artistically with the appropriate feeling and expression.

A state-supported school (particularly outside the United States) or a major preprofessional training program will usually follow one of the aforementioned methods of training or a similar curriculum. Students who wish to attend one of these schools must audition for acceptance. During the audition process, each prospective student is evaluated according to body proportion, flexibility of the joints (especially their legs and back), arched feet, muscle tone, and natural coordination. This helps to ensure the successful completion of the dancer's training. These students take ballet classes on a daily basis, and the syllabus for each successive year sequentially incorporates more steps from the ballet vocabulary with increasing difficulty, whereby over a period of years the young dancer is sufficiently trained and prepared to enter a ballet company.

The majority of ballet teachers in America do not teach in a state-supported or preprofessional setting; they are more likely teaching in a studio that has an eclectic assortment of body types and multiple levels of talent and ability. The class will mostly have students who are there for the recreational enjoyment of it, and perhaps just a few will have career aspirations in dance. Also, as previously stated, a teacher's method of training may reflect an eclectic approach and style because so many ballet teachers in America and Europe have trained in an eclectic mixture of methods; only a relatively small percentage have completely studied within one formalized system. And for those teachers who do come from one system, they may not be teaching in a pedagogical setting that comfortably supports the strict adherence to that method.

It is important for teachers to establish semester or year-end goals and objectives for each level of technique that are reflected in some type of formulated syllabus with accompanying lesson plans of their own design or of the school where they teach. Without this, teachers have no road map or structure to follow that intelligently guides them through the year.

Training goals are the broad areas that eventually produce a fully trained dancer. They remain throughout one's student years and professional career, though some may be emphasized more than others by different teachers. These goals are, in part, posture and placement (balance), strength and flexibility, coordination, vocabulary of movement, elevation, speed and technical precision, fluidity of movement, purity of line, musicality, artistic expression, and knowledge of ballet—past and present—and fostering an appreciation of ballet. Teaching objectives are the specific tools that will successfully accomplish these goals. They are primarily the steps, plus the technical canons and use of musical and artistic emphasis, that you will use to formulate your syllabus, construct your exercises, and build your lesson plans.

It is a worthwhile exercise for teachers to examine the architecture in a series of their lesson plans and identify whether the instructional objectives are reaching the desired goals. For instance, two or three *allegro* combinations in less than 15 minutes will not accomplish one's goal of increased elevation, and absence of slow and sustained movement in the *adage* at the barre and in center floor will not develop balance and build strength.

Each of the aforementioned systems of training, whether it is an actual curriculum or not, puts forth objectives to be accomplished in a given period—the training goals are implied. When the lesson plans are methodically designed and taught effectively, the goals become self-evident. Knowing these goals and having access to any one of these syllabi will be extremely helpful as a reference point or guide to developing your own syllabus. Absent this, you will have to construct your own. This chapter is your guide on how to do this.

༄༅

Designing a syllabus for children's classes (ages 5–7 pre-ballet, and 8–10 formal ballet) will be more simplistic, and it will have a slower rate of progression than a syllabus for adolescent/adult classes simply based on bone and muscle development and coordination and cognitive factors. A good deal of time will be spent at the barre along with being seated on the floor in pre-ballet.

During early adolescence in girls (puberty) and later adolescence in boys, growth spurts can complicate a student's progress because muscular development usually does not keep up with quick bone growth. This does not necessarily call for adjustments in the syllabus unless most of the students are going through it, but it does present a temporary, albeit frustrating, problem for a student's improvement to which a teacher should be sensitive.

Plan and begin your syllabus by mapping out what you want and realistically expect to achieve within the designated proficiency level of a children's or adolescent/adult class: Beginner I and II, Intermediate I, II, III, Advanced I and II, or Pointe, etc. This should be planned over a predetermined number of weeks that correspond to a semester, the entire year, or any other calendar division. Establish specific steps and movements you consider are sequentially appropriate for that class level based on what they have already learned, or refer to the appropriate lesson plan or syllabus of one of the established training methods as a guide. Knowing what students have previously learned is important, and it is easy if the students are being promoted in levels within the same school. Students coming from a different school should always be admitted into a new class with the agreement that s/he may have to be moved into another level.

Your next step is to divide the semester or calendar division into smaller teaching units or blocks consisting of four, six, or eight weeks (again, depending on how many times per week the class meets). Multiply the weeks plus the number of times the class meets per week to determine the total number of classes for that unit. Map out what you think you can realistically accomplish from the beginning to the end of the unit time based on your syllabus. Then begin to construct your lesson plans based on that mapping. Don't be overly aggressive in developing a syllabus, as students need time to perfect their technique. Keep your students challenged but not overwhelmed. Remember that a new class should always build on what was taught in previous classes. This means either giving selected steps and combinations from preceding classes, or repeating the most recent class, and modifying it gradually with the introduction of new movements. Some steps are more difficult than others to perform correctly, so those should be repeated class after class.

Designing a set barre that can be given over a period of weeks or even the semester—with some variations as needed—will prove valuable because it will free up more time to give center floor exercises and combinations.

Lesson Plan

The lesson plan is the architecture of the ballet class, and it reflects the specific objectives that will accomplish one's teaching goals. Within this architecture there should always be sequential progression. Sequential progression can be used in multiple contexts in ballet training. It refers to how a lesson plan is designed in terms of the logical sequencing of the barre exercises and center combinations, which is shown later in this chapter. Similarly in that context, sequential progression means that each lesson plan should have a logical and intelligent connection to the next class, and so on.

Sequential progression also means teaching certain basic steps that are required before more difficult and technical steps can be given. To identify what these underlying steps are requires a methodical breakdown of the more advanced step. Let's take *brisé* as an example. It is a jump, and it begins and ends with a *demi-plié*, it requires a *dégagé*, and it is a jump from one to two feet as in an *assemblé*. It is also a beating step, and so, along with the above prerequisite steps, basic beats (particularly *entrechat quatre*) should be taught before introducing the *brisé*. The prerequisite steps for teaching beats—*entrechat quatre, trios, six,* etc.—are *sous sus, sauté, soubresaut, changement, temps levé, échappé,* and *échappé battu.*

Before any turns such as a *pirouette* or *piqué/chaîné* can be learned, the student must be taught how to spot. Spotting might be taught by skipping or doing triplets diagonally across the floor and adding a two-part turn consisting of a quarter turn followed by a three-quarter turn while incorporating the correct coordination of the head and eyes in spotting. Along with spotting, *relevé* and *retiré* must be taught before a pirouette is given and *posé* before a *piqué* turn. Analyzing each new step that is to be taught will signal to the novice teacher what prerequisite steps have been taught and what remains to be covered in the lesson plan to properly prepare the students.

A lesson plan reflects an individual lesson with its progression of the barre and center floor work. It can be either an outline or a comprehensive notation that incorporates complete exercises and combinations. Lesson plans can be different for each class that is taught for an advanced or professional level, but the wisest teaching approach for a less advanced level is to use the same lesson plan with few variants for multiple classes (3–4).

Very often I observe professional teachers who have a helter-skelter way of teaching. Their class lacks overall structure and an intelligent sequential progression within the lesson plan as well as from class to class. Each day is a new lesson without any connection to the previous day's class. That combined with a pacing deficiency often results in whole sections of a class being left out, such as adagio or grand allegro.

The general goals in your syllabus as well as the specific exercises in the lesson plan should be balanced in terms of variety of movement and time allotted to each section of the class. There are seven movements of ballet. These can be very helpful to reference as the divisions or sections of the barre and center floor are being planned. All dance movement, including the seven movements, can be broadly categorized as axial and locomotor—steps that are stationary and those that move through space, respectively.

Plier	To bend
Relever	To rise
Étendre	Stretch
Glisser	To glide
Tourner	To turn
Sauter	To jump
Élancer	To dart

In addition to the seven movements of ballet, there are eight classical positions of the body and five arabesques, as found in the Cecchetti (Italian School) Method and the ABT National Training Curriculum.

Croisé devant

À la quatrième devant

Écarté

Effacé

À la seconde

Épaulé

À la quatrième derrière

Croisé derrière

The French and Russian schools use the above positions but add to them: *écarté derrière, effacé derrière,* and *épaulé derrière.*

Fig. 2.1. *Croisé devant.*

Fig. 2.2. *À la quatrième devant.*

Fig. 2.3. *Écarté.*

Fig. 2.4. *Effacé.*

Fig. 2.5. *À la seconde.*

Fig. 2.6. *Épaulé.*

Fig. 2.7. *À la quatrième derrière.*

Fig. 2.8. *Croisé derrière.*

Fig. 2.9. First *arabesque*.

Fig. 2.10. Second *arabesque*.

Fig. 2.11. Third *arabesque*.

Fig. 2.12. Fourth *arabesque*.

Fig. 2.13. Fifth *arabesque*.

Gail Grant's *Manual and Dictionary of Classical Ballet* is an excellent reference for classical ballet vocabulary. It should be part of every teacher's collection of dance reference books.

Classes should **not** be regarded as separate entities; rather, they should build on the previous classes and always be in tune to the importance of continuing repetition of the designated steps.

Often teachers are more ambitious than what their students are capable of doing, and revisions are in order. The preferable scenario, of course, is when a class of students excels beyond expectations. In either case, be prepared to make modifications throughout the individual class as well as with future classes because not all students have the same learning curve and will not progress at the same rate. Many schools have enrollments where within the same class level there are varying percentages of students who take one or two classes per week and others who take five or more classes per week. This will affect the rate of progress for that class level over a given period.

Most important, don't rush or be rigid in your lesson plan. Let your students' overall learning curve set the pace for the term, not what you have determined for your goals and objectives in your syllabus. Be flexible and allow yourself to take more time on something if you feel it is important and will ultimately benefit your students and accomplish your overall objectives. Don't progress too fast if most of your students are still struggling with the material you have given them.

Remember, it takes seven to nine years of daily training to bring a student to the level of advanced/professional. It is absolutely imperative for students to develop correct habits of muscle memory in posture and placement and accurate execution of technique. Therefore, allow them the time to get it right!

Constructing Your Class

The structure and language of a ballet class are universal. One can go anywhere in the world to take class and expect barre work to contain certain prescribed steps: *plié, tendu, dégagé, rond de jambe à terre, fondu, frappé, développé, petit battement, rond de jambe en l'air, grand battement.* Center practice will have *adage/balances*, various types of *pirouettes* and turns, *petit and grand allegro*, and traveling movements across the floor such as a waltz, *piqué turns*, or *grand jetés*. How certain exercises and combinations are structured and sequenced will vary from teacher to teacher. For example, a teacher may begin a barre with a simple *tendu* or some series of therapeutic movements prior to a *plié* combination, give the *pirouette* section before *adage*, and perhaps finish the class with *batterie* instead of *revérence/port de bras*. But these are minor structural differences. The essential overall structure and vocabulary of a ballet class remain consistent.

Important goals of the dancer are to build strength and flexibility while refining and perfecting technique. It is a slow and arduous process of repetition over many years, and success depends largely on the structure of the classes and the effectiveness of the teacher. Major teaching impediments to building strength and technique include the following:

1. Constructing combinations that are unnecessarily complicated and making them difficult to memorize. All too often, teachers choreograph their classes, constructing long combinations that have far too many steps. The student perfects a step through repetition, and time should be spent doing just that, not expending unnecessary energy memorizing long choreographic sequences. It is always better to give shorter exercises and more of them than a long choreographic variation.

2. Failure to give an adequate number of jumps, which are extremely important for building muscle strength as well as bone tissue.

3. Rushing through class—the failure of the teacher to allocate enough time to methodically guide students through the execution of a step. Therefore, it is important to keep your lesson plan simple and uncomplicated. A sufficient number of individual steps and combinations can be given along with time to work on them if they are of simple design, which allows them to be quickly taught and memorized.

Plan your classes so they have a sense of continuity and progression from one class to the next, or teach the same class for a period, making just simple modifications or introducing a new step. This is particularly important when teaching children and beginning students. Students usually remember what the teacher gave during the last class, and they enjoy having the opportunity to work on the same step or combination in the subsequent classes. Obviously, time does not allow you to cover everything from your previous class and also introduce new work. But you should reinforce some of the steps, especially from center floor work, that build on more advanced steps. I have watched teachers time after time give a class that has no intelligent connection or continuity to anything they did in their last class. This is confusing and counterproductive for students. Even when I teach an advanced/professional level on a daily basis, I will repeat selected combinations. As the combination is familiar to the dancers, they don't have to expend time and energy memorizing; they have the opportunity to concentrate fully on perfecting their execution of it and, for allegro, reversing it. And believe me, dancers like that.

The most valuable and desirable qualities that a director or choreographer looks for in a dancer are cleanliness and precision in technique and an unmannered simplicity of style and line, thereby allowing the specific style of the choreography to come through. Avoid stylistic flourishes and affectations when you are teaching and demonstrating, and discourage these things if your students incorporate them into their dancing.

೦৲৯

The ballet class is divided into two sections: a series of barre exercises followed by center floor work.

Beginner and children's classes usually are scheduled for 1 or 1¼ hours. The amount of time devoted to barre and center can vary a great deal depending on the lesson plan and how much has been learned to date. On occasions a greater proportion of time might be spent at the barre, especially with beginners or when new steps are given, as most ballet steps are first taught at the barre before proceeding to the center floor. But it is important for students—children and beginners—to experience movement in the center and across the floor.

Intermediate through advanced levels are traditionally scheduled for ninety minutes to two hours. Ideally, the 90–minute class should be divided into thirds: 30–40 minutes for barre, 25–30 minutes of center floor for *adage* and turns, and 25–30 minutes for jumps. Teachers often find it very difficult to teach a full barre in just 30 minutes. It is possible though when you have a set barre (same exercises) or when you combine multiple exercises.

Once ballet basics including barre work have been taught, the focus of class should be on the center floor work, where students truly learn to dance—to balance, turn, jump, connect steps, and move powerfully and gracefully through space. This is where the whole vocabulary of ballet resides. The purpose of the barre work is simply to prepare the dancer in all the various ways for work in the center. Therefore, it stands to reason that once basic fundamentals have been taught, more than half of the class time, if not two-thirds of it, should be spent perfecting movements of the center floor. (Often I observe teachers unnecessarily spending an hour or more at the barre teaching intermediate and advanced students. Consequently, they are then unable to get more than three or four exercises completed in the center and are not able to give a complete class. The emphasis on the barre work is clearly misplaced.)

Barre work has several purposes:

1. Warm the body and make it supple—generating heat through increased circulation in the muscles and fascia along with stretching and increasing the range of movement in the joints and spine.

2. Placing the body, i.e., establishing correct posture through accurate alignment of the musculoskeletal structure along the vertical axis or line of gravity, and establishing placement (balance & counterbalance) in axial and locomotor movements.

3. Practice of basic positions, *port de bras* and *épaulement*, movement isolation, and multiple movement coordination of upper and lower body incorporating the practice and understanding of biomechanical movement as the foundation of fundamental balletic movement. Most center floor steps will first be taught at the barre.

4. Build strength and flexibility in the legs, feet, and torso—especially through the back and core center—while maintaining and strengthening the turn-out. (Stressing the building of strength should always be balanced with stretches to maintain flexibility.)

5. Prepare the dancer for the center floor lesson plan. (Structure certain barre exercises so they prepare the student for what you will be giving in the center floor.)

Sequencing the Barre Exercises

The order in which barre exercises are given differs slightly between the training methods that represent the French, Russian, and Italian schools. However, all of them begin with *plié* followed by exercises that address principally the foot and ankle. It is after dégagé exercises where sequencing begins to differ. There really is no right or wrong to the sequence. Construction of the barre should be dictated more by the design of individual exercises or combinations and how intelligently they fit together as a complete barre.

There is a helpful guiding principle to follow (though it is not a hard and fast rule) when sequencing your barre. It is to alternate the strenuous large muscle group exercises where the leg is 90° or higher with small muscle group exercises, usually involving the foot and lower leg. For example: giving a *battement frappé* in between a *développé* and *rond de jambe en l'air* combinations, or giving a barre stretch or *petit battement* combination between an *adage* and *grand battement* exercise.

Of course, what is considered a strenuous exercise to some is not to others. The overall strength and technical ability of a class of students is a helpful barometer. The factors that determine a heavy or strenuous exercise are the intrinsic technical difficulty of a movement, how much continuous work is done with one leg, the length of the entire combination and whether there are any resting points such as *port de bras or cambré*, and finally, the tempo. Giving back-to-back exercises involving primarily large muscle groups is perfectly acceptable if the above criteria are factored in while you design them. The barre should definitely build strength, yet not be so difficult and over-the-top that your students feel depleted before coming into center floor. There were many of us professional dancers in New York who used to say about a famous teacher that "if we can make it through Madame's barre, we can make it through anything!" So use your common sense when constructing your barre exercises and learn how to **read** your students. I find, sometimes humorously, that dancers have quite a repertoire of facial and body language nuances that communicate how they feel during and after a combination they find extremely difficult and heavy.

Here is one example of a barre sequence. It is similar to the Russian School.

1. *Demi* & *grand plié w/port de bras*
2. *Battement tendu*
3. *Battement dégagé (glissé)*
4. *Rond de jambe à terre*
5. *Fondu développé*
6. *Battement frappé*

7. *Rond de jambe en l'air*

8. *Petit battement*

9. *Développé/adage*

10. *Grand battement*

It is beneficial for your students if you can incorporate a barre stretch into the sequence of exercises whenever possible in addition to various *port de bras/cambré* movements within various barre combinations. A stretch combination can be given during the latter part or end of the barre.

Traditionally, barre begins with a *plié* combination. However, many teachers prefer to begin with a simple *tendu* in first position (often facing the barre) as the initial exercise to establish the dancer's center alignment. Over the years, therapeutic pre-barre warm-up sequences have emerged as the preferred start of class. Joanna Kneeland's Therapeutic Barre was done at the start of each ballet class during the late 1960s and early 1970s at the Harkness Ballet School in New York. This type of warm-up has great merit, but it also takes up a lot of the allotted time for formal barre work. So I leave that decision up to the individual teacher.

After the start of the formal barre executing the *plié*, the foot is the next point of concentration for the following three or four combinations of *tendu* and *dégagé*. The barre should gradually proceed to incorporate exercises that fully engage large muscle groups of the legs, back, and pelvis including warming the muscles around the hip joint. It is also beneficial to incorporate into some combinations a full range of movement involving torso flexion, extension, and rotational bending that will stretch and elongate the spine and coordinate head and arm movements through *cambré/port de bras.*

As with center floor work, barre exercises are learned gradually and layered into its complete sequential progression. The complete barre sequence may seem like too many exercises to accomplish in 30–40 minutes, particularly for the beginning teacher. It takes practice and experience to teach and deliver a class succinctly and to keep a steady and consistent pace, but if exercises are kept simple, they can be quickly demonstrated and easily memorized. Sometimes it is necessary to combine multiple steps into your *enchaînement,* such as a *frappé* with *petit battement* or the *adage* with *rond de jambe en l'air.* Keep in mind, however, that when multiple steps are combined, they become more complicated.

Lastly, a word about the traditional language of classical ballet. It is so important that students learn the French terminology of ballet—pronunciation, meaning, and spelling. This should begin at the children's level, teaching one or two terms each week and requiring students to keep a terminology notebook.

Barre Exercises

Plié

Plié (bend) is the most important movement we have in ballet. Practically every step begins and ends with it—we simply could not dance without it. The *plié* is a movement, not a position; it is what a dancer moves **through** in order to get into the next step or directional change. **Feeling** the *plié* is very important, but getting **stuck** in it is another matter.

As a beginning exercise, it consists of a complex set of motions that enable the dancer to feel movement of the entire body, especially when it is done with *port de bras/cambré*. It establishes the initial feeling of posture and placement—the center line of gravity (the plumb line)—and it incorporates movements of the ankles, knees, and hip joints, the release and rotation of the legs (turnout), and the alignment of the torso over the legs and feet (base of support). Incorporating stretches going forward and sideways (flexion), backward (extension), and circular (rotation) simultaneously enables the spine to become warmed, stimulated, and stretched.

The *plié* exercise can begin in first or second position. I recommend that it begin in second position and then proceed to first, fourth, and fifth. (Note: Beginning students are given *grand plié* sequentially in first, second, third, and fifth positions before introducing fourth position.) Beginning in second position allows the dancer to feel maximum use of the turnout with the heels firmly down and grounded during the first *grand plié*. It also allows maximum use of turnout with easier flexion in the hips and stretching through the groin while pressing the knees out and in alignment with the feet. The spine, head, shoulders, and rib cage maintain vertical alignment while the pelvis stays level. Overall, it is a steady, firmly grounded, and comfortably balanced position to begin barre work.

Common errors: sitting at the bottom of the bend and going too deep. The pelvis should stay slightly higher than the horizontal level of the knees (never below), and the movement should be a smooth, continuous, even movement on the descent and ascent. In *grand plié*, the heels (except in second position) should lift only as much as they have to, and then press into the floor as soon as the ascent begins.

The *plié* exercise gives the teacher her/his first opportunity to watch and guide the dancer into correct body alignment and balance. Unfortunately, there are many dancers—students and professionals alike—who regard the *plié* as their own loosey-goosey pre-barre warm-up, which somehow implies permission to drop the chest, pitch the back, sit at the bottom of the bend, and be generally off-balance while camouflaging their skeletal (mis)alignment with multiple layers of wooly warm-ups. It is exasperating to many of us teachers! Students should be encouraged to come to class early enough so they can do whatever personal warm-up they feel is necessary. As for all of the excess bulky warm-up clothing, students should be reminded that warming the body happens from the inside out, not the reverse.

Tendu

Tendu (stretched) works the foot while lengthening and stretching the entire leg. The action of the *tendu* should establish a straight line from the hip to the toes while the leg stays isolated from the hip joint, with no movement in the pelvis. It strengthens the ankle and instep and develops the necessary tactile sensations and articulation of the sole of the foot against the floor, which is crucial in *allegro* steps.

The *tendu* can be done with the accent timing in or out or even and with various accompanied movements: *plié, fondu, chassé, temps lié*, etc.

Common errors: placing weight onto the working leg and toes; curling toes under instead of stretching/lengthening them, especially in fourth *derrière* position; allowing the foot to sickle and letting the toes come off the floor.

Dégagé

Dégagé (disengage), also called *glissé* (glide) and *battement jeté* (throw), is a much stronger action of the foot than a *tendu*. It, too, has an extended feeling through the entire working leg, isolated from the hip joint, but here the foot comes off the floor anywhere between 20° and 45°. It has a much stronger dynamic action than a *tendu*, and the accent timing can be in, out, or even.

Dégagé helps prepare the student for the needed speed and correct execution of all *allegro* steps that have a beginning outward brush of the working foot such as *jeté, assemblé, glissade*, and *brisé*.

Common errors: allowing the foot to sickle; leg too high—above 45°; losing control of the turnout, especially when closing in fifth position; and allowing the pelvis to tilt or displace in fourth *devant* and *à la seconde*. In fourth *derrière,* the pelvis must adjust when the leg goes above 15°, which will also require a slight forward adjustment of the torso.

Rond de Jambe à Terre

Rond de jambe à terre (round of the leg—circle) is the first really complex exercise after *plié*. It is a circular movement of the leg that loosens and warms the hip joint, strengthens turnout, and establishes a rotary isolation of movement in the working leg. The working leg must remain fully stretched, as in a *tendu* position, equally distanced from the supporting leg throughout the *en dehors* and *en dedans* circles. The working foot must move through the fully extended *tendu* fourth *devant, à la seconde,* and fourth *derrière* positions. When brushing through first position, the working leg remains stretched and the foot remains level with the floor. *Rond de jambe à terre* can be done with the toes slightly off the floor (*en l'air*), but only after correct technique of doing it *à terre* has been firmly established.

Rond de jambe à terre prepares the student for many steps that require a circular movement of the leg, including *pas de basque, grand rond de jambe en l'air, grand battement arrondi,* and *renversé relevé* and *sauté*.

Common errors: loss of turnout in the working leg while moving from side to back and in the upper thigh of the supporting leg; loss of leg isolation by allowing the hips to move when circling the working leg; bending the working knee and letting the working foot roll in while brushing through first position; and foreshortening the working leg.

Fondu

Fondu (sinking down) is simply a *demi-plié* on one leg. The quality, however, is that of softly melting or stretching. It is one of the most important placement exercises in ballet and should be given not only during the barre but also as a center floor exercise. *Fondu* prepares the student for controlled takeoff and landing for jumps as well as slowly descending on one leg from *pointe*. It is one of the more complicated movements to teach initially because it usually involves the coordination of both legs moving simultaneously while maintaining correct placement (balance) over the supporting leg. Both legs must bend into the *fondu* and then extend to straightened legs. Prerequisite positions and movements as *cou-de-pied, développé,* and *enveloppé* should be taught prior to introducing *fondu.*

Common errors: not maintaining the center line of balance over the arch of the foot; misalignment of the knee to the turned out foot (loss of rotation in the supporting thigh) in both a *fondu adage* exercise and landing from a jump; and not working the legs simultaneously.

Frappé

Frappé (struck) calls for a strong percussive brush against the floor with the toes and ball of the foot. It strengthens the ankle, calf, and foot—particularly the intrinsic muscles around the metatarsals, which stretch and point the toes. These muscles can only be strengthened by resistance striking or brushing against the floor. *Frappé* begins in *sur le cou-de-pied* position, which has variations (wrapped, flexed, and fully pointed) according to which school or tradition of training is being followed. Proper execution requires that only the lower leg—knee down—shows the action while the turnout of the working thigh is maintained and its shape remains relatively still. *Frappé* is the foundation for *jeté.*

Common errors: ending the brush with a sickle foot; moving and losing the rotation in the working thigh; and failing to strongly brush or strike the floor. Some teachers do not teach the brush against the floor but teach to the point *tendu* instead. This really defeats the purpose of the *frappé.*

Rond de Jambe en l'Air

Rond de jambe en l'air (rond de jambe in the air) should first be taught at 45° so that the circular action of the lower leg can more easily be controlled before proceeding to 90°. The pattern of movement is a half circle that takes place from the knee down. There is a slight rotation in the knee joint, being that it is a modified hinge joint (see chapter 3). Starting with the leg in second, when done *en dehors,* the knee bends as the foot makes a straight line toward the side of the knee and then draws a slight half circle forward (away from the center of the body) to finish fully extended to the side. *En dedans* is the reverse pattern: the foot draws a slight half circle inward (toward the center of the body) to the side of the knee followed by a full extension of the leg to the side. The foot never travels behind the line of second position (i.e., behind the knee). Since the action of the *rond de jambe en l'air* is of the lower leg, the thigh remains stationary and rotated.

Rond de jambe en l'air is an excellent movement for building leg strength while controlling movement of the lower leg and flexibility of the knee joint. It can be done in center floor *en relevé* or *sauté,* and it prepares the student for more advanced *allegro,* such as *gargouillade.*

Common errors: allowing the thigh to drop below the 90° starting level; doing a full circle with the lower leg, passing the foot behind second position; and losing the turnout of the working thigh.

Petit Battement

Petit battement (small beating) is similar to the *frappé* in that it is done *sur le cou-de-pied* and the action is from the knee down while maintaining control of the working thigh. It prepares the student for all *allegro entrechats,* beating the legs with accuracy and speed. The pattern of movement is straight to the side with an in/out action of the lower leg, moving out just far enough for the foot to pass from *devant* to *derrière.* It is easier learned with the toes or even the ball of the foot on the floor, so your students have the tactile sensation of the movement direction.

Common errors: if there is any tension in the knee, the thigh will tense and the action will move from the hip joint instead of the knee; the knee rolls in, losing turnout in the working thigh; the in/out movement becomes slightly circular instead of straight.

Développé/Adage

Développé (developed) builds strength and coordination in the legs as well as balance and control in the spine and torso. The eight classic directions of the body are refined and strengthened utilizing the *développé* through each of them, particularly when the extension of the leg is held for a time. It begins from a *retiré* position of 45° (for beginners) or 90° and unfolds to the same level as the knee in *retiré.* A good deal of strength and control is required through the torso/pelvic placement for 90° and for higher extensions where the thigh must be lifted from the hip joint preceding the *développé,* and the lower leg must then come evenly to the set level of the knee and thigh.

There is less hip and spine displacement in *devant* and à *la seconde* than in *arabesque,* where the hip begins to tilt when the leg goes above 15°. In this position, precise counterbalance is needed in the torso and position of the arms to maintain correct placement.

Développé can be combined with other movements to create an *adage: demi* and *grand rond de jambe, battement passé développé, tire-bouchon, penché, grand fouetté,* etc.

Common errors: letting the thigh turn in when going into fourth *devant* and *arabesque*; extreme displacement of the hips—tilting and twisting—and rounding of the spine. Most problems are associated with placement.

Grand Battement

Grand battement (large beating), like the *développé*, builds strength and coordination in the legs as well as balance and control in the torso. It is a strong percussive kick to a high extension followed by a steady controlled descent using eccentric contraction in the thigh muscles. Teachers often explain this movement by saying, "*Battement* the leg up freely, but carry it down with control." When first taught, the accent is **out**. Once the student acquires the requisite strength to control his/her center of gravity and the deep muscles of the spine, pelvis, and abdomen, the accent can change to **in**. This makes the up-and-down dynamics of the *grand battement* quite strong, preparing the dancer for the large beating action *cabrioles* as well as for all steps involving a full range of movement in the leg.

There are many variations of *grand battement*. It can be done from fifth position to fifth position, from point *tendu*, or as a *grand battement développé, grand battement arrondi, grand battement en cloche* or *balançoire*, etc. Nearly all *grand allegro* steps require a *grand battement: grand jeté, grand jeté en tournant, saut de basque, grand fouetté, grand cabriole, temps de flèche,* etc.

Common errors: because the leg is thrown to its highest level and requires the pelvis to tip, students will often make the following technical errors: lifting the working hip in anticipation of the *battement à la seconde* instead of as a result of the leg ascending, allowing the working hip to move forward with the leg in fourth *devant* instead of keeping the hips square and firm, and anticipating the forward lean of the torso in *arabesque* before the *battement* leaves the floor. Other faults are loss of turnout and those found with the *développé* placement errors.

Stretching

Full barre and floor stretches can be given once the back and large muscle groups of the legs and hips have been thoroughly warmed. They can be given before the *adage* or *grand battement* or at the very end of the barre. With more advanced classes, the teacher will let each dancer do her/his own sequence of stretches. Stretching is important in order to maintain the balance between strength building and flexibility. Hyperflexible dancers, usually girls, need to stress strength development, so stretching should be carefully monitored and often minimized with them (see chapter 4).

Center Floor Work

The ballet barre prepares the dancer for center floor; it is in center where the student learns to dance. The center floor work, being the primary focus of the ballet class, is divided into sections beginning with *exercises au milieu* or center practice followed by sections of adage, turns, petit allegro, and grand allegro. Traveling steps consisting of turns, jumps, waltzes, etc., that make full use of the studio space should be integrated into one or two combinations when possible with each class. The level of technical difficulty and comprehensiveness of the exercises will run the gamut from simplistic gallops and *balancé* waltzes for children's classes and beginners to more complicated and demanding combinations for preprofessional and professional levels.

Always set your objectives and plan your class according to what you want to do with center floor work. Begin at the end and work backward. That way you can intelligently plan your beginning center floor work to support the allegro sections and the *barre* exercises to support your entire center floor lesson plan.

Center Practice

The first one or two exercises should be simple axial or stationary ones that allow the dancers to feel their placement and balance without the support of the barre. This is usually an exercise that was done at the barre, e.g., *tendu, dégagé, frappé, rond de jambe à terre,* or *fondu.* It can incorporate various *relevés, pas de bourrée,* and even simple turns. *Temps lié* is a particularly good exercise because it requires changing the center of balance from one leg to the other while feeling the connective movement through the *plié.*

In children and adult/adolescent beginner classes, the center floor work in the beginning will mostly consist of exercises that were done at the barre, e.g., *plié, tendu, dégagé, rond de jambe, relevé, pas de bourrée,* followed by simple jumps and locomotor movements across the floor that include gallop, polka, *pas de basque*, and *temps levé*.

Adage

Adage/*port de bras* can be as basic and as simple as a coordinated *port de bras* done with a *retiré développé* in an *en croix* pattern for the beginner, to a more extensive adage that includes *promenades*, *penché*, balances, and various turns and transitional movements for the intermediate and advanced students.

Adage is immensely important because it is here that the dancer refines *port de bras*, *épaulement*, and purity of the classical line. Nearly every component of turns and jumps can be practiced and perfected in a slow and controlled way. By working *à terre* (on the ground) and incorporating *fondu*, one can develop the strength, control, and coordination to do the same step *en l'air* (in the air).

Practically everything that a dancer does in an *adage* can be converted to and executed as a turn or a jump. For example, let us look at a simple first *arabesque* and a few of the movements we execute in this position during *adage*: *promenade* and *fondu* prepare the dancer for *arabesque turns* and for the landing in *arabesque* in jumps such as *grand jeté* and *grand jeté en tournant*. It can be taken further into a *fouetté relevé arabesque*, which contains all the technical mechanics for a *grand fouetté sauté arabesque*; instead of pushing the floor away for the *relevé*, one thrusts downward into the jump, while the coordination of the arms with the legs remain the same. So to reiterate, whatever you eventually want to do *en l'air*, you should first teach *à terre* through *adage*.

Turns

Turns include *pirouettes en dehors* and *en dedans*, *arabesque*, *attitude*, *à la seconde*, *soutenu*, *fouetté*, *piqué*, and *chaîné* turns, etc. In more advanced classes, many types of turns can be incorporated into the *adage* work, especially *arabesque*, *attitude*, *à la seconde*, *and pirouette en dehors* and *en dedans*.

Every class should include traditional *pirouettes en dehors*. From there you choose which additional turns to do according to your teaching objectives and lesson plan for the term based on the class level. You can revisit execution of turns (*piqué*, *chaîné*, *emboîté*, etc.) later when the class begins to travel across the floor.

Allegro

The allegro portion of center floor is of primary importance and should demand a major portion of the allotted lesson time, 25–30 minutes of a 90–minute class. After all, look at what percentage of the ballet vocabulary consists of jumps. These are given in the latter part of the class and, unfortunately, due to poor planning and/or pacing, jumps are often given in the final 10–15 minutes of class. Not nearly enough time to cover an adequate variety of jumps with time to repeat and/or reverse combinations.

> Allegro is the foundation of the science of the dance, its intricacy, and the bond of future perfection. The dance as a whole is built on allegro.
> (Agrippina Vaganova, *Basic Principles of Classical Ballet*)

Allegro steps are divided into three basic categories: *petit* or small, medium, and grand allegro. Tempo, more than the individual step itself, plays the defining role for small and medium jumps.

Petit allegro includes jumps *terre à terre* where the feet barely leave the ground, along with small quick jumps without a lot of elevation. Medium *allegro* often consists of the same steps as *petit allegro,* but it is done to a slower tempo or a different rhythm or meter, which allows time for more sustained dynamics and elevation. Whether stationary or traveling, small or medium size steps, quick or moderate tempo, *allegro* must always be done with precision footwork and brilliantly dynamic legwork in *batterie.*

The repertoire of jumps falls into certain descriptive categories depending on the takeoff and the landing of the step. The following are the various categories of jumps along with a few examples:

1. Two feet to two feet (*sauté, changement, échappé*)
2. One foot to one foot (*jeté, glissade, temps levé*)
3. One foot to two feet (*assemblé, brisé*)
4. Two feet to one foot (*sissonne*)

The first allegro exercise should be a series of jumps from two feet to two feet. These are usually just simple *sauté, échappé, changement,* etc. Never give advanced or heavy steps that take off or land on one leg as a first jump combination (e.g., *brisé, cabriole,* or *brisé volé*). *Petit allegro* combinations should start out simple and build in difficulty.

Some of the more common steps that would be given for the *petit allegro* section of the class, depending on the level of advancement, would be *jeté, glissade, assemblé, sissonne, brisé, pas de chat, ballonné, ballotté,* and *cabriole* in all the various directions, as well as stationary jumps, such as *échappé sauté, changement, soubresaut,* and *entrechat trios, quatre, cinq, six.* There are many steps to learn and perfect in *allegro*; enough time should be allotted to do a minimum of four or five exercises in every class. Keep them simple so they are easy to teach, learn, and memorize. Always teach each step individually until it can be done with an acceptable degree of precision before combining it with other steps to form a more complex combination.

Grand allegro. These are big jumps that are usually traveling and covering a large area of space. Students love this part of the class where they have the opportunity to move across the whole studio floor. They can be done on the diagonal across the studio, *de côté* (side to side), upstage to downstage, or *en manège* (in a circle). Some of the more common steps that are done in *grand allegro* are *grand jeté, grand jeté en tournant, saut de basque, saut de chat, faille assemblé,* and *grand fouetté sauté. Grand allegro* steps should also be taught individually before combining them and incorporating more intricate connecting movements. At least one *grand allegro* should be given in a class.

Movement *en Diagonal*

Movements that travel on the diagonal usually consist of turns such as *piqué, chaîné, emboîté* or a waltz, and *chassé coupé.* In more advanced classes, such movements can be combined with *grand allegro,* such as *piqué* or *chaîné* turns combined with *chassé coupe jeté en tournant.* Movements *en diagonal* as with *grand allegro* give students the opportunity to move expansively over a large area of space and are among the more enjoyable sections of the class. It is energizing and fulfilling. This part of class is very important, and teachers should make an effort not to neglect it. Often teachers do not pace their classes well enough, and as these combinations come at the end of class when time is running out, either they are not done or they are rushed.

Révérence

This is certainly optional. Many teachers do not do it, but I find that it is a calm, culminating, and aesthetically pleasing way for students to end their class time. There is an atmosphere of completion—of closure. Students traditionally applaud at the end of the class as an acknowledgment of respect to the teacher. In many schools, the students come up one by one to thank the teacher, whereby the teacher can also acknowledge the accomplishments of each student's work.

Pointe Work

Incorporating *pointe* work into ballet technique class will vary according to the level of advancement and how many classes are taken per week. It is sometimes given at the end of class for the final 15 to 20 minutes, or as a half-hour addition. If there are boys in class, they will be given men's steps, such as double *tours* and *à la seconde pirouettes* alternating with the girls' *pointe* exercises. This, of course, will change the amount of time normally allocated for the barre, center practice, and *allegro.*

In preprofessional upper division classes, the center floor, or the entire class, can be danced *sur le pointe.* There are differing attitudes as to whether barre work in an ordinary technique class should be done *en pointe,* because the shoes do not allow the feet to work with the range of flexibility that should be practiced. I leave that up to the individual teacher and dancer. Classes structured solely for *pointe* work and offered once or twice per week, augmented by a certain amount of *pointe* in regular technique class, make for a well-rounded curriculum.

⁓

There should always be a logical and consistent connection between the barre and the center floor work. Whatever you plan to teach in the center floor technique should be integrated, whenever possible, within the appropriate barre exercises and in the beginning center work.

Here are a few simple examples:

- Stressing the position of the working leg and the placement over the supporting leg in the landing and takeoff in *jeté sauté* in the center can be addressed at the barre in *relevé plié* on one leg and in *fondu développé* exercises.
- The inward action and accent of various *batterie* requires strong and accurate sideward *tendu* and *dégagé* exercises with the accent "in."
- Accent "in" on *grand battement* to a strong musical march accompaniment will support the teaching of *cabriole* in the center.
- When *fouetté* is included in the center floor lesson plan, include it in the barre exercises.

Notating Your Class

Having a lesson plan that outlines the contents and sequence of the class is enough for some teachers, while for others a more entailed notation is needed. Writing down your combinations and exercises for class is a good idea in the beginning for new teachers. It is an expedient method for memorizing the class, and it will reveal whether a combination is evenly phrased musically.

I remember my dear friend Woytek Lowski telling me when he was ballet master for American Ballet Theatre that he wrote out every combination the night before he was going to teach morning company class. He trained as a dancer in Russia at the Kirov, where he also received his teaching certificate from the Vaganova Choreographic Institute. Woytek was an excellent teacher and very popular among the ABT dancers. But since he had only recently retired from dancing and begun working full-time as a ballet master and teacher, he felt more confident when he walked in to teach if he wrote down the class beforehand in his notebook.

After more than 25 years of teaching, I continue to write down certain combinations that I feel are particularly well structured and musical and have worked well for the particular needs of the dancers.

It is not really practical to notate all of your classes when you are teaching multiple classes every day. It is valuable, though, to have a notating method so that you can refer to certain combinations—particularly center floor work—for your week-to-week classes. If you aren't teaching the same students on a nearly daily basis, it is difficult to remember combinations you gave to a particular class a week ago. Notating is also an excellent way to perfect your spelling and learn the definitions of the French ballet vocabulary—something that should be taught to all young ballet students.

There are many ways to write down your class. I recommend that every teacher develop his/her own method, one that you can quickly refer to and easily read, preferably at a glance. Develop your own abbreviations for right and left, forward and back, leg and foot, arm and head, etc. Use the various classical positions, such as *croisé devant, effacé,* or *écarté,* and directions of movement: the eight directions of the square and theatrical stage directions (upstage, downstage, stage right to left, and so on) and their abbreviations.

If you are rusty when it comes to your French ballet terminology, I recommend that you brush up. It will make your notation much easier, and your students will benefit that much more by hearing you use it and requiring them to learn it.

The following examples of notation layout are a guide for developing your own system.

Adage (3/4 meter)
(16 measures)

Legs and Feet	Arms and Upper Body	Counts or Measures
right foot (r/ft) 5th position, devant croisé	5th position en bas/ port de bras 1st to 2nd	4 meas. Intro (5–6–7–8)
retire développé r/lg croisé devant, fermé 5th	croisé devant	1–2–3–4
retiré développé l/lg to croisé arabesque fermé 5th	croisé arabesque	5–6–7–8
retiré développé r/lg écarté devant	écarté devant	1–2–3
pivot to effacé devant	effacé devant	4
plié piqué arabesque and fondu	1st arabesque	5–6
pas de bourrée under to	2nd to 5th en bas head	7–8
5th position croisé	en face	

Here is another example, using a different format that is more of a longhand notation. The counts are in parentheses, and I put a double slash after each set or phrase of 8 counts so I can easily check that my phrasing is even (8, 16, or 32 measures of music). Brackets are placed around the notation that pertains to the upper body—arms, head, and *épaulement*.

This is my personal choice of notating because, if it is written completely but succinctly, I can visualize it more easily because it usually flows and has a better sense of continuity. However, it is more difficult to use at a glance.

RL=right leg	DS=downstage	DSR=downstage right
LL=left leg	UP=upstage	DSL=downstage left
RA=right arm	SR=stage right	USR=upstage right
LA=left arm	SL=stage left	USL=upstage left

Petit Allegro (quick 3/4 meter—waltz)

RL 5th devant en face [en bas]. Temps levé chassé pas de bourrée right [1st to 2nd] (1–2); 2 pas de chat (3–4) [RA 4th en avant]; repeat left (5–8) //. Temps levé chassé pas de bourrée right [1st to 2nd] (1–2); 2 jeté over [*4th* en avant opposite arm to working leg] (3–4); two assemblé over [2nd] (5–6); 2 changement de pied [2nd to finish en bas] (7–8) //.

Piqué/Pirouette (2/4 meter—rag)

RL tendu croisé devant [RA, 4th en avant]. 2 piqué turns on diagonal DSR (1–2); chassé pas de bourrée to 4th pos. plié, en face (3–4) [2nd to 4th prep]; single pirouette en dehors fermé 5th devant (5); double pirouette en dehors from 5th (6); close RL 5th in plié, croisé derriere (7); straighten to LL tendu croisé devant (8). Repeat other side.

For those teachers who are ambitious about reading and writing notation, there are formal systems for notating dance movement. They are extensive and thorough, and any one of them will take much time and effort to learn, as well as being expensive. They are used primarily for notating choreography and are not always conducive to notating daily classes because of their time-consuming and comprehensive nature. Perhaps a slight exception to this may be Valerie Sutton's Sutton Dance Writing®. She offers a Dance Writing Shorthand that can be learned using her website.

Labanotation is the most commonly used system in the United States for notating dance movement and choreography. It is written vertically in two columns for right and left. Labanotation can be learned through the Laban Institute in New York.

The Benesh Movement Notation system is commonly used in the United Kingdom and British Commonwealth. It notates dance movement on a musical five-line staff. RAD syllabi are notated using Benesh, as is the repertoire of the Royal Ballet. I have yet to meet any teachers who teach using a formal notation system.

3

Anatomy for the Dancer

A classroom combination or piece of choreography can be danced in many ways by altering the elements that create quality of movement: time, space, energy, phrasing, style, focus, aesthetics, etc. One teacher may request a step to be executed in a particular way, while another wants the same step danced differently. Perhaps the difference is based on the rhythmic quality of the chosen music (elements of time and energy) or on the teacher's own training style and development as a professional dancer. Nevertheless, the principles of correct technical execution of ballet are based on proper anatomical placement and the laws of physics. It is the utmost responsibility of all teachers to safeguard these principles.

Every ballet teacher should have a fundamental understanding of the musculoskeletal system and the biomechanics of human movement as it pertains to dance. S/he should always teach technique with a sound anatomical approach. Precise execution of a movement requires correct technique, which in turn requires accurate posture and placement in balancing and counterbalancing. This is paramount because once muscle memory—physical habit—is established through repetition, it is difficult to undo. Unfortunately, many studio hours are spent retraining dancers and breaking bad habits in technique, placement, and *port de bras*.

Anatomy books have been written for dancers and teachers that should be on every teacher's bookshelf for easy reference. The purpose of this chapter on anatomy is to reinforce and emphasize important points regarding muscular and skeletal functions as they apply to correct dance training as well as to highlight certain areas that are particularly vulnerable to dance injuries.

The Dancer's Foundation

The ultimate goal of every well-trained dancer is the ability to perform any step in classical ballet or stylistic choreography with grace and aplomb while expending the least amount of energy. Correct posture (stance) and placement are the primary elements of a dancer's technical foundation. Dancers gradually develop strength and muscle memory during years of training that enable them to control and coordinate these elements through balance and counterbalance while executing stationary, traveling, and transitional movements. Therefore, the first fundamental responsibility of every teacher is to cultivate a solid training foundation for the student that will develop and maintain correct posture and placement.

Posture is the dancer's erect and evenly balanced preparatory stance, usually in first or fifth position, both at the barre and in center. It represents correct skeletal alignment, especially regarding the spine. The skull, shoulder girdle, ribcage, spine, and pelvis are held in vertical alignment, and they are equally balanced over the legs and feet without undue muscular tension or gripping. If we could see our skeleton in this stance through our skin and musculature, it would look similar to the skeleton we saw hanging from the crown of its skull in our high school anatomy classroom or in our doctor's office. The spine is elongated with its natural curves, and the head and torso are in vertical alignment over the pelvis. The pelvis is balanced equally on top of the legs and feet.

We define placement when we move out of a postural stance into a pose or sequence of movements that require a redistribution of weight in order to maintain correct balance. To understand the concepts of balance and counterbalance through posture and placement, it is helpful to identify (1) each of the three body planes, which link two of the three dimensions of height, width, and depth, (2) the center of gravity, (3) the central vertical axis, and (4) the base of support.

The coronal (vertical) plane is a vertical line that divides the body into front and back parts. When viewing this line from a profile position with the feet in parallel, it runs from the top of the head, just in front of the ear, continuing through the pelvis, hip joint, and knee, and into the metatarsal

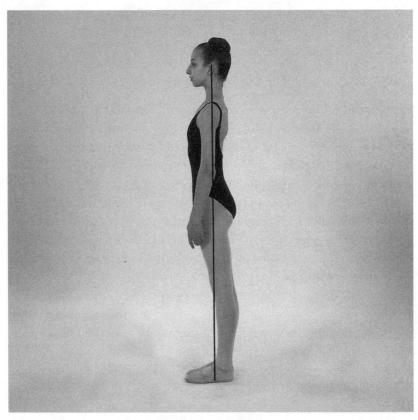

Fig. 3.1. The coronal plane.

or transverse arch in front of the ankle. The spatial dimensions in movement are height and width, as in a stretch or *cambré* to the side or a cartwheel (fig. 3.1).

The sagittal plane is a vertical line that symmetrically bisects the body into right and left halves. When viewed from the front with the feet in first position, this line runs from the top of the head through the center of the body ending between the heels—the base of support for the evenly distributed gravitational weight of the body. The spatial dimensions in movement are height and depth, as in a forward bend or backbend or a somersault forward or backward (fig. 3.2).

The coronal and sagittal planes together establish the central vertical axis, also referred to as the line of gravity or the plumb line.

The horizontal (transverse) plane divides the body into upper and lower halves. The spatial dimensions in movement are width and depth (rotation) as in a *pirouette* or *fouetté* turn. The point at which all three planes (coronal, sagittal, and horizontal) cross each other is the center of gravity (COG)—the imaginary point where all parts of the body balance each other. This is located just below the navel at the body's midline and anterior to the second sacral vertebra (fig. 3.3).

When a dancer transfers his/her weight from two legs to one from first position, a transfer of weight must take place. The line of gravity and the base of support between the two heels are repositioned over to the transverse arch of the supporting foot. However, when the feet are in fifth position, the line of gravity already runs through the transverse arch, and there-

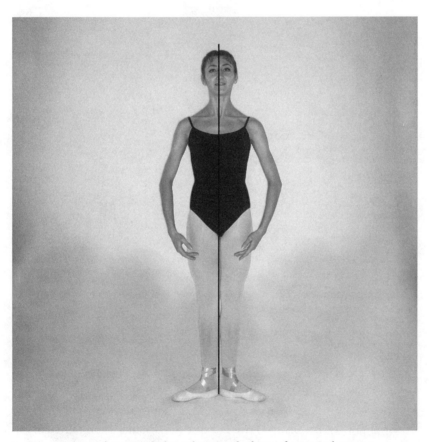

Fig. 3.2. The sagittal plane showing the base of support between the feet in first position.

Fig. 3.3. Central vertical axis (combined coronal and sagittal planes) intersected by the horizontal plane. All three planes intersect at the center of gravity.

fore no shift of weight is necessary when going from two legs to one (figs. 3.4 and 3.5).

Correct ballet posture and placement also require elongation through the legs and torso by means of lengthening and stretching. This is universally known and often misunderstood as pull-up. Elongating the body raises the center of gravity. By raising it, we increase the distance from our center of gravity and our base of support on one or both feet. It is done by lengthening and stretching the spinal column, thereby elongating the spine's natural

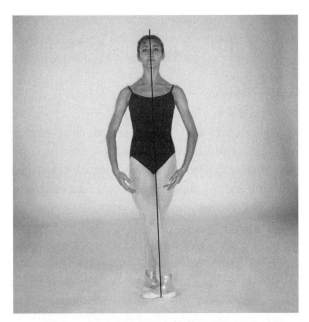

Fig. 3.4. Plumb line (central vertical axis) in fifth position
and the base of support at the transverse arch.

Fig. 3.5. *Développé à la seconde* showing the plumb line or vertical
axis running through the torso, supporting leg, and transverse arch.

curves. This causes diminished stability, but enables greater mobility, allowing the dancer to move with speed, lightness, and grace. The diminished stability factor is overcome by years of muscular development and control while refining technique.

Two oppositional forces should be felt with elongation, raising the center of gravity. There should be a sensation of pushing downward through the legs from the hip joints while lengthening and pulling up from the waistline. Upward elongation of the torso from the waist should be felt primarily in the spine with a slight expansion sideways in the rib cage. The head, neck, shoulders, and arms should remain free of any tension. Maintaining this stance requires core abdominal strength as well as control in the upper back between the shoulder blades.

A common error often occurs when students apply a directive to pull up. The usual anatomical point of reference for this is the front of the torso—the stomach, ribs, and sternum. When they lift up from these frontal points, it causes the lower ribs to lift and flare outward, creating a pigeon chest appearance. This in turn causes the spine to slightly arch and the shoulders to adjust backward, which incorrectly alters the line of gravity.

The correct feeling of pull-up from the waist should be felt as a lifting or lengthening of the whole spine including a feeling of elongation through the neck. Both sides of the waistline just above the pelvic crest are good reference points for sensing the lift or pull against the downward pushing of the legs. It also engages the abdominal muscles and properly expands the rib cage outward to the side, thus allowing for proper diaphragmatic breathing.

I should point out here that my choice of words for the explanation of raising the center of gravity is for adolescent and adult students. Such words as *pull-up, elongation,* and *lengthening* are too abstract for children and will not make sense to them. They need to be taught using words and images that are appropriate for their age, such as "stand up very tall," "push the floor away," and "grow taller."

Recapping, posture is defined as the dancer's stasis vertical stance in one of the five positions. When it is done correctly, there is a feeling of balance and composure, and only minimal energy is expended.

The art of ballet requires dancers to move with grace, speed, balance, and aplomb. Difficult and technical movements must be performed in an efficient manner and with the look of ease, rather than showing how difficult a step is and how much energy is being expended to accomplish it. Dancers strive to perform each and every step using economy of effort, that is, using the least possible amount of energy. The way to accomplish this is through correct anatomical balance. When the body maintains proper balance or counterbalance in movement, the least amount of energy is expended. Being off-balance requires more energy to stabilize and control movement.

Placement is differentiated from posture by movement and corresponding counterbalance. Whenever the torso changes positions or there is a weight transfer from one leg to the other, the vertical axis changes correspondingly. Placement is the continual redistribution of weight between the head, torso, pelvis, arms, and legs in relation to the vertical axis and center of gravity while in the act of moving or in stationary positions. The use of the arms, or *port de bras*, is an important factor for placement coordination—maintaining stability and equilibrium as well as creating a look of symmetry with the head, legs, and torso. As with correct posture, precise balance in placement will give a look of ease to positions and movements and will not require an excessive amount of energy to perform them (fig. 3.6).

Fig. 3.6. Placement in *arabesque* showing the correct counterbalance of the working leg, torso, and arms in relation to the center of gravity and over the base of support. Notice how the *arabesque* is visually and aesthetically balanced.

Too much weight in one direction will cause a loss of balance or require the dancer to exert more muscular strength and energy to save or control a movement or position. This gives the step a labored and uncomfortable look and causes muscular tension and gripping. It also places stress on the joints, ligaments, and tendons, which over time can result in stress injuries.

There are two important factors that can impact posture and placement: turnout and visual focus.

Improper or forced use of turnout can cascade into many different technical flaws and eventual injuries. Principally, it can tilt the pelvis and move the spine, thereby altering the center line of balance. It can also displace the alignment of the hip joint to the knee and the knee to the ankle joint.

How the eyes function in dance is extremely important, and too often they are ignored during training. The eyes serve a dual purpose in dance. First, they are one of three centers that supply proprioceptive information to the brain, letting it know our body's relative position in space. (The vestibular and somatosensory systems are the other two.) Our proprioceptive balance system is responsible for maintaining our body's center of gravity. For example, if we take our gaze below eye level, dropping the horizon line, the body's tendency is to adjust by leaning forward. And if we lift the gaze above the horizon line, the adjustment leans backward. Many young students tend to lift their eye level when trying to hold a balance or lifting their center of gravity higher. This usually places them slightly back and off their center of balance.

Second, the eyes project the line and direction of movement and usually anticipate any directional change. Focused vision is a natural sensory/somatic function that ties closely to proprioceptive equilibrium. When one simply walks down the street and changes direction or turns to speak to someone, the eyes initiate the change of direction with the turning of the head followed by the body. Likewise in dance, the eyes and head generally lead unless *épaulement* or choreographic design dictates otherwise. They should always remain consistent with the traditional and correct position and line of the whole body. The eyes also project energy—magnetism—which projects dance across the footlights to the viewing audience. As I stated in the introduction, students have the bad habit of getting their eyes stuck in the mirror rather than following through the line and direction of movement. Therefore, paying attention to visual focus is as important as attention to a pointed or unpointed foot.

The Spine and Skeletal Alignment

The overall function of the bony skeleton is to support our body's weight against the force of gravity. The principal function of our spine is to support the weight of our head and the torso while transferring that weight into the pelvic bowl where, with the help of numerous crisscrossing muscles, it is evenly distributed onto the legs. The relationship of the spine (weight bearing) and the pelvis (weight distribution) to the legs constitutes the major process of balance and counterbalance in dance positions and movements. Moving the spine off the vertical plane changes the line of gravity and affects the center of gravity. We continually do this as we move from one position to another.

Flexibility of the spine is essential to a dancer's ability to move choreographically with aplomb. Therefore, it is important to properly and thoroughly warm and stretch the group of muscles that run alongside the spinal column (*erector spinae*), which then activates the synovial fluid in the vertebral discs. This is as important as the attention we give to the feet, ankles, knees, and hips at the start of barre. Right from the beginning and throughout the barre, the structure of the class should always include flexion, extension, and rotation, which incorporate the full ranges of directional movement in the spine.

The spinal column is divided into four main sections beginning from the base of the skull: cervical, thoracic (also known as dorsal), lumbar, and sacrum/coccyx. It can move in four directions according to the type of vertebrae: forward flexion, extension (backbend), lateral flexion, and rotation. With the exception of the sacral vertebrae, which form the back of the pelvis and are held tightly together by strong ligaments, the spine has the ability to move in two or more directions. It is helpful to know these directions when adjusting a student's position during a stretch.

The cervical vertebrae have the ability to move in all directions: forward and back (flexion/extension), side to side (lateral flexion), and by rotation.

The thoracic vertebrae can move with lateral flexion and rotation, but little or no forward flexion or extension.

The lumbar vertebrae can move with forward and lateral flexion plus extension, but have little or no ability to rotate.

Students sometime experience pain or discomfort in their lower lumbar and sacral area after doing a lot of extension stretching or when their leg has been held for a long time in *arabesque*. Stress is placed on the ligaments that hold the five fused sacral vertebrae when a backbend is done while the legs are fully turned out or working in an *attitude derrière* or *arabesque*. If pain and discomfort develop, it might be wise to keep the legs parallel during any backbend stretch or completely avoid doing full backbends or high leg extensions to the back until the source of the discomfort is identified and the pain subsides.

There are three major curves in the spine: cervical, thoracic, and lumbar. These curves along with the vertebral discs function as shock absorbers. By lengthening or elongating these curves, we strengthen the spinal column and diminish the vulnerability to spinal injury. Additionally, elongating raises the dancer's center of gravity and enables one to move with greater speed, mobility, and lightness. Hence the ubiquitous directives: "pull up," "grow tall," "lift your center," "lift out of your hips." These directives range from being beneficial to innocuous to often misinterpreted, which can result in lifting the lower ribs and inflating and jutting out the chest, pigeon breast style. This causes the spine to curve more and therefore shorten.

Conversely, it is important to maintain enough degree of curves in the spine so that the shock of landing in a jump is absorbed there and not transferred to vulnerable joints such as the ankles, knees, and hips. Some teachers mistakenly think that the spinal curves must be completely eliminated.

It is crucial for teachers to stress the importance of feeling length in the spine before doing extensions—full backbends—or lifting the leg into *arabesque* or *attitude*. Otherwise, too much stress is placed on the lumbar vertebrae, which will cause injury to the spinal discs over time.

There are two ways in which to move the spine: directly and indirectly by moving the pelvis. The sacrum is attached to the pelvis at the sacroiliac joint by very strong ligaments that do not allow the sacrum to move independently of the pelvis. Actively tilting the pelvis in standing posture—tucking under or standing swayback—or passively moving it as a result of doing a *grand battement* or *développé* alters the placement, shape, and curves of the spine.

Although the spine is located close to the center of the torso, we often reference it from behind because we can see and feel the bony knobs of the vertebrae (transverse processes). This is acceptable because viewing and correcting placement is often performed best from the back. When the lengthen or pull-up directive is given, it is beneficial to stress the image of being long in the back, equally long on the sides, and slightly short in the front, thereby keeping the rib cage in correct alignment while lengthening the spinal curves. Lifting from the front will usually cause the back to shorten and arch.

The dancer's stance or posture should be natural, following the line of gravity (also referred to as the plumb line or central vertical axis). Viewed from the side, the line runs from the top of the head down in front of the ear, through the pelvic crest, hip joint, and knee joint, in front of the ankle, and into the transverse arch of the foot. Viewed from the front or back, this line equally bisects the body; the head should be balanced symmetrically on level shoulders, shoulders and rib cage in vertical alignment, with the spine placed on top of the level pelvis and with the pelvis symmetrically balanced on top of the legs.

The pelvic bowl distributes weight equally onto the two standing legs. When the center of gravity is positioned low, we have the quality of looking more weighted and grounded, and when it is high, we have the quality of lightness. Modern dance makes use of weight and plays more with the center of gravity at different levels. There is a natural tendency for the body to allow the center of gravity to return to its natural position. In ballet, we are usually trying to keep it raised—a constant process. When the center of gravity is lifted and sustained, the dancers can shift weight and balance from one leg to the other with great speed, mobility, and aplomb.

Placement through the Feet

Where the weight is placed on the feet, and particularly when standing on one foot, is a much debated topic among teachers and dancers. It is true that dancers dance on the balls of their feet, making sure that their weight stays forward and not back into their heels. So often I have watched dancers during barre bounce lightly on the balls of their feet and go through an exercise with their heels slightly off the ground. I feel this is a mistake and the wrong approach to feeling light and ready to take off, not to mention the strain and gripping that happens in the foot and ankle as a result of the heel being off the floor. The feeling of lightness should be maintained by pushing into the floor and lifting the center of gravity, and lengthening the legs while keeping the heels in contact with the floor.

In correct stance, the weight of the body is equally distributed onto the foot in a triangular pattern between the first and fifth metatarsals and the heel. Between these points lies the arch, bracing and supporting that weight. This is where the weight should naturally be when standing on the flat foot and when landing from a jump. But because our weight can easily settle back on the heel when we are fatigued and drop our center of gravity—thereby making it difficult and cumbersome to move quickly and accurately—we anticipate and compensate for this by trying to keep our weight slightly forward toward the ball of the foot. This is where trouble and misunderstanding for the dancer begins.

Whenever the adjustment of weight toward the ball of the foot is required, it should be minimal, only what is necessary. Perhaps the ball of the foot is not the best anatomical reference point; instead, it should be the transverse arch. The dancer should always feel that the entire foot is supporting one's weight through the arch and that it is sufficiently anchored into the floor. In order for the foot to be strong and powerful, especially in the takeoff thrust and controlled landing of a jump, it must experience force and resistance against the floor. Once compensation to the ball of the foot goes too far, weight goes completely off the heel, causing a number of problems: it alters the center line of gravity, displacing skeletal alignment, which then must be held in its off-balance position by gripping muscles; the vertical line of the straight supporting leg is diminished or even at a diagonal angle, which often results in sitting into the hip; and the heels are unable to meet and feel the floor when taking off and landing from jumps, putting undue stress on the Achilles tendon, which could eventually cause tendonitis (and usually does).

Two of the five functions of the foot are propulsion and shock absorption. The foot is the last part of the body that propels the dancer into a jump, and it is the first to absorb the initial shock of the landing, working sequentially from the toes, metatarsals/ball, and heel. But often dancers fail to bring the landing through the center of the foot, especially when landing on one foot (or when doing a *fondu*). This pitches the weight forward onto the ball of the foot and the knee beyond the toes and prevents the heel from contacting the floor. Therefore, it is a good training approach to stress the importance of the landing positions. This can best be done while giving *à terre* movements such as *fondu*.

There is a lot of choreography that does not allow dancers the time to get their heels down or to execute technique correctly. But choreographic demands performed onstage should not dictate how dancers work in class. Daily class is the time to perfect and reestablish technical precision and define classical line and quality of movement.

Muscles and Stretching

Muscles move, control, and stabilize our skeleton. They propel our body into movement as well as slow it down and stop it. They also stabilize the body in both stasis posture and dynamic movement and balances. Muscles have three basic characteristics: they stretch, they contract, and they are elastic—they will return to their original length after being stretched. Muscle tissue turns into tendons toward the end of the muscles, and these strong semi-elastic tendons attach the muscles to the bones. Glide your fingers down your calf muscle toward the heel, and you can feel how the muscle begins to narrow into the Achilles tendon, which attaches the calf muscle to the heel.

Muscles are made up of bundles of fibrous tissue encased in connective tissue called fascia. Some of the fascia fibers are gelatinous. When the body is cold, these gelatinous fascia fibers are also cold, making the muscles feel tight or stiff. Once the body warms up, the gelatinous fibers soften and flow, thereby allowing a greater and safer range of motion while stretching.

Increasing or maintaining flexibility through stretching is important, and how much and what type of stretch will depend on the individual needs of each dancer. Too much stretching, particularly if it involves ligaments, can result in hypermobile or loose joints, which will increase the risk of injury. Unlike muscles, ligaments are not elastic, and once they are stretched, they will not return to their original length.

The two types of stretches that dancers do regularly are static stretching and dynamic stretching. In static stretching, a position is held for 20–30 seconds, such as remaining in a split or straddle on the floor. Dynamic stretching is done while moving, such as doing a forward bend, an arched stretch to the side, a backbend, or a *penché*. It is never a good idea to do ballistic stretching, and students should be cautioned against this. Ballistic stretching is when one bounces while in the stretch. It risks tearing muscle or fascia tissue. Doing proper stretches that involve a maximum range of motion and, therefore, a definite feeling of resistance reflex in the muscles should always be done after the body is warmed up.

Teachers and students should remember that strength and flexibility must have a balanced relationship. Having a loosey-goosey body may be great for high leg extensions, but it requires a good deal of muscular strength to control such hyperflexibility.

Nearly all of the stretching that is done in ballet either directly or indirectly involves the spine by arching side or back (*cambré*), bending forward, or rotating. Therefore, the act of lifting or lengthening the torso, especially the upper back, prior to entering into the movement will elongate the spine, giving a fuller stretch with a greater range of movement and a more aesthetic look.

Incorporating the use of breath is an important element to the mechanics of stretching, use of *port de bras*, and balletic movement in general. Unfortunately, teaching students to be aware of how they breathe and knowing how important breathing is in dance has diminished over the years. As the science of Yoga has become more mainstream in the West along with its teachings on the use of breath in stretching, more and more dancers are now learning and benefiting from it. Generally, we should use inhalation to elongate the spine and begin the movement, and we should use the exhalation to move us further into the stretch or to increase and deepen the stretch once we are there, thereby helping to relax the reflex response in the muscles. We use the inhalation again to bring us out of the stretch. The exception is the backbend, which should be done with an inhalation moving into and out of the arch and exhaling toward the end of the recovery movement.

Every dance movement that is performed has a dynamic to it, which means that there is a particular degree of intensity and velocity to the directional flow of energy. A movement is given a certain quality—through dynamics—and is transformed into art through the use and manipulation of energy. The breath is one of our most tangible references for energy, and it is an integral part of physical expression and the projection of choreographic movement.

The Mechanics of Breathing

Holding or contracting the core abdominal muscles is one way dancers are taught to control their center of gravity. As a result, they often constrict the rib cage and prevent themselves from breathing fully; they breathe only in their upper chest region, which is known as chest breathing. This certainly is not the best way to breathe and to fully oxygenate the blood for optimal muscle response. The best way to breathe is diaphragmatically. Unfortunately, the technique and benefits of diaphragmatic breathing are rarely taught or fully explained to students.

The diaphragm is a dome-shaped muscle that separates the heart and lungs from the lower digestive organs and functions as the major muscle of respiration. It covers the entire inner circumference of the rib cage and attaches to the rib cage and the first three lumbar vertebrae. During full diaphragmatic inhalation, the diaphragm contracts, moving downward, and its form flattens into a rounded disclike shape. At the same time, the internal and external intercostal muscles of the rib cage and lumbar spine are activated—outwardly expanding the side of the rib cage and lengthening the spine. As a result, the lower lobes of the lungs draw in more air and a greater volume of blood is oxygenated, which gives the dancer better muscle response. As the lungs exhale, the diaphragm relaxes upward, returning to its dome shape. So teaching students to either expand the rib cage to the side on inhalation or breathe from the solar plexus will properly activate the diaphragm and fully expand the lungs. Over time, this will increase lung capacity and strengthen the dancer's stamina, along with helping the dancer to maintain the lengthening of the torso.

Developing Muscle Memory

As the function of the skeleton is to support our weight, the primary function of muscles is to move the bony skeleton via the joints. Reflex control, or muscle memory, is the unconscious synapse of engaging a group of muscles to perform a certain task. It is an automatic function in the brain as a result of constantly repeating and reminding the muscles to engage in a certain way. Establishing reflex control, such as maintaining control of the abdominal muscles while dancing, requires constant attention and reminding from the teacher until the process happens automatically, unconsciously. Establishing and maintaining control of center placement—the line of gravity—becomes part of the dancer's muscle memory over time. One of the anatomical reference points for this is the abdominal region, one's core.

There is also an important second reference point for maintaining correct posture and placement that is often forgotten. It is the upper and middle back between the shoulder blades and down to the last (12th) thoracic vertebra. It is there that the two core muscles known as the psoas are attached. The psoas muscles have important functions: they are directly involved in transferring weight from the torso to the legs and feet, and they stabilize the spine and function as the principal hip flexors. Maintaining control of the back at that point between the shoulder blades, with a vertically placed spine, will help keep the pelvis correctly positioned and will allow the abdominal muscles to engage properly. Additionally, this will maintain a lifted sternum and will keep the chest open and broad. So, with a teacher's directive to engage the abdominal muscles, it should also include awareness of control in the upper/middle back.

The Knee Joint

The knee joint causes more trouble to dancers and athletes than any other part of the anatomy because its very structure is prone to injury. The knee is constantly engaged when we dance, whether the movement is locomotor or stationary. The knee is a hinge joint that moves forward and back (flexion and extension), but unlike other hinge joints, its structure allows a slight rotation, making it easy to destabilize and vulnerable to injury.

When the knee bends slightly, as in a *demi-plié*, the medial and lateral ligaments on either side of the knee joint become lax, which allows for a small degree of rotation—moving side to side—and this makes the joint unstable. There is a slight inward rotation when straightening and locking the knee and an outward rotation when bending.

As the knee is bent, it can easily twist out of its alignment with the thigh and foot, causing injury to ligaments or cartilage. Misalignment due to extreme rotation, whether violent or repetitive, will cause injury. Therefore, it is imperative that the dancer maintains correct torso placement along with alignment of the thigh, knee, and foot, particularly on the takeoff and landing of jumps.

Fully straightening the knee, by pulling up the thigh's quadriceps and drawing the medial and lateral ligaments taut, will align, lock, and stabilize the joint. This is why fully straightening the knee at the end of circling the knee joint in a *rond de jambe en l'air* is so important. Strengthening all the muscles of the thigh gives greater stabilizing control over the action of the knee.

Swayback Knees

Hyperextension in the knees contributes to a beautiful line of the legs when working *en l'air,* but it can create problems as a supporting leg with balance and placement. The common error is sitting into the back of the knee instead of standing with a straight, pulled-up vertical leg. When this happens, the knee becomes passively locked in this position, and there is little or no engagement or lengthening through the quadriceps. There is a tendency for the dancer's weight to fall back from the center of the arch onto the heel, distorting the vertical line of balance, which gives a bowed look to the leg when viewed from the side. To compensate for the displaced weight to the heel and the feeling of sitting back, the student may pitch her/his weight more toward the ball of the foot, thereby distorting the vertical line of the leg even more and further exacerbating the placement distortion by sitting into the supporting hip. S/he then finds it difficult to *relevé* from a straight leg because the weight of the body is not running in a straight line of gravity to the foot and into the floor.

The only way that I have found to correct this, in my own dancing and that of my students, is to work with visually straight legs, making sure that the kneecap and quadriceps are pulled up. At first it may feel to the dancer as if s/he is working on bent knees, but that's all right. It's illusory: the knees are, in fact, straight and properly engaged. (Whenever a habit—reflex control/muscle memory—is corrected, reprogrammed, it will feel wrong because it will be out of the realm of the dancer's comfort range.)

The Foot

The ballet dancer's feet are the most amazing and complex part of the anatomy. They are trained and developed to perform with nearly the same degree of articulation, sensitivity, and dexterity as the hands.

There are five ways in which the foot functions:

1. Weight bearing
2. Propulsion (e.g., jumps)
3. Lifting (e.g., *relevé*)
4. Shock absorption (e.g., landings)
5. Non-weight bearing (e.g., flexion, *frappé*)

As previously stated, weight displacement is triangularly supported between three points of the foot: the forward part of the heel and the first and fifth metatarsals (ball of foot). Within this area is the transverse arch—base of support. On the sole of the foot are four intrinsic muscle layers that have multiple functions:

- They help the foot to be grounded to the floor.
- They assist with lifting and propulsion.
- They maintain the arch of the foot and control the working shape of the ballet foot.

Strongly pointing the toes, thereby giving added propulsion, as the feet leave the floor in a jump is done by these sole muscles. Because they do not cross over any major joints, the only way they can become strong and powerful is by working the foot against the floor through resistance—the actions of brushing, pushing, and striking. Teachers can never stress this too much when students do *tendu*, *dégagé*, and *frappé à terre*, as well as when jumping.

Going onto the Toes

It is the dream of most girls in ballet class to go on their toes. I dare say that many of the mothers of these girls are equally as eager and will often pressure the teacher to allow their child to go on pointe before she is ready.

It can become a sticky ethical and business situation when there is an ultimatum such as "The dance school across town said they will put my daughter 'on toe.' This means so much to her, and if your school is unwilling to do so, well, I suppose we will have to think about changing schools." This scenario usually happens when the child is both too young and anatomically underdeveloped or when strength and properly developed technique are missing.

The benchmark age for a girl to go on pointe is 11 or 12. It has long been believed and accepted that until this age the bones of the foot have not sufficiently ossified into hard bone tissue capable of bearing the weight in executing pointe work. The sports medicine community is now beginning to doubt and dispute this rubric, but what is not in doubt is that it still takes three to four years of concentrated training before a girl has the strength and technique to go on pointe. So if the child begins ballet at the correct age of 8, she will be 11 or 12 after she has the prerequisite years of training.

The occasional student who is registered for one ballet class per week and probably misses about every fourth or fifth week is not an eligible candidate for pointe. Once the student goes on her toes, she should be taking at least three ballet classes per week. Needless to say, pointe should only be for the serious dancer.

The feet and ankles must bear an enormous amount of pressure when standing on pointe. Great pressure is exerted on the knees, hips, and lower back, requiring sufficient counter strength in the legs, abdomen, and back, along with controlled turnout of the legs from the hip joints. Strong and secure placement must be evident; otherwise, serious damage of the soft tissue can occur, and those injuries may not manifest until years later. Whatever the student will be expected to do during her beginning pointe work, she first must be able to do it correctly on the *demi-pointe*.

There is a wonderfully informative pamphlet published by Capezio Dancewear entitled *Why Can't I Go on My Toes?* It is an excerpt from Celia Sparger's book, *Anatomy and Ballet*, where she clearly explains the development of the foot (including X-rays) and what is required of the student before pointe work can commence. I recommend that teachers keep a few copies on hand to give to all eager, persistent, and insistent mothers and pupils.

The All-Important Turnout

The movement vocabulary of classical ballet is designed to be performed utilizing the outward rotation of the legs, or turnout. While certain steps can be accomplished with little turnout, more complex steps cannot. Technically and aesthetically, classical steps will not have the correct and desired look unless they are done with an adequate degree of rotation. Assuming there is no skeletal impediment to one's turnout, developing as much flexibility in this part of the anatomy of the young dancer is as important as developing strength in the legs, feet, and torso.

Ligaments bind bone to bone at the joints. The insertion of the femur into the pelvis is a ball-and-socket joint that is held by these strong ligaments. Unlike muscles, ligaments are tough and do not stretch easily. Care must be taken to gradually stretch them incrementally, not forcibly. Unlike muscle tissue, ligaments that are overly stretched will not return to their original length; therefore, it is important to simultaneously build supporting strength in the muscles (principally the rotators) that stabilize and have a direct relationship to the hip joint. Building strength and flexibility together should be accomplished through a balanced approach. In cases where turnout is severely limited, pointe work should never be encouraged.

Turnout originates in the hip joint. The angle of the upper thigh (femoral neck) and the directional opening of the hip socket (acetabulum) play a major role in determining the allowable degree of turnout. Some students have a skeletal structure that allows little or no rotation, and no amount of stretching will significantly alter their ability for turnout. A medical examination with X-rays can determine the significance of the problem. Depending on the severity of this angle/orientation and resulting degree of limited rotation, some will find it difficult or nearly impossible to correctly execute classical ballet movement.

Working the Turnout

Newton's Third Law of Motion states that "for every action there is an equal and opposite reaction." Dancers know this, experientially, better than most. In order to move, force must be exerted and met by equal resistance. This is constantly in play in all upright stationary and locomotor movement—the pushing force against the resisting floor. Likewise, working the turnout must be done using oppositional force—both legs simultaneously rotate outward in opposition to each other. Concentrating on the turnout in the working leg without engaging turnout in the supporting leg (emphasizing the top of the inner thigh) will not increase, strengthen, or stabilize the overall turnout (fig. 3.7).

Alignment of turned-out legs, thigh/knee/lower leg/foot, must be maintained in order to avoid injury, particularly to the knee. A 180° rotation rarely, if ever, happens completely from the thigh and hip joint, especially in third and fifth positions. Rotation of the front thigh in fifth position is usually 60° to 70°. The remaining rotation happens through the lower leg and rotation in the ankle, completing the look of 180° in both legs.

This remaining rotation of the feet through the lower legs and ankles should not be encouraged with young children; their feet should maintain

Fig. 3.7. *Tendu à la seconde* showing the oppositional opening or rotation of both legs beginning from the upper thighs.

a straight alignment with the thighs and knees. As the student develops strength and flexibility in the feet and ankles, the fifth position adjustment can gradually be made to complete the correct finish of the turnout. At that time, careful attention should be paid to the fully turned out fifth position, making sure that the front foot does not pronate and roll in and that the knee is not twisted or strained (figs. 3.8 and 3.9).

Anatomy for the Dancer   75

Fig. 3.8. Correct fifth position.

Alignment of the foot and ankle in all positions is extremely important. Rolling in of the feet is a very common problem for young dancers as they try to gain more turnout in the legs (fig. 3.9). Musculoskeletal misalignment, especially in the feet, can lead to acute and chronic injuries. Rolling in and rolling out can sometimes be revealed by looking at the student's ballet shoes. The shoe will ride up on the foot from the outside or inside, respectively.

Notice that when the feet are turned out completely in fifth position with straight legs, the front knee is not in line with the toes. When the dancer goes into *plié*, however, the strongly held turnout is released in the hip joint; the thighs and knees can then come into alignment with the feet. But this releasing of the turnout places the dancer in a precarious position, especially

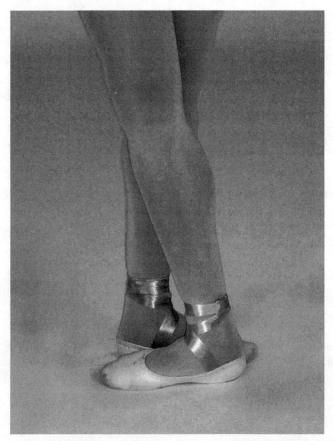

Fig. 3.9. Incorrect fifth position with a rolled-in front foot.

when landing from a jump on one leg, because if the thigh and knee are not in proper alignment, there is great risk of injury to the knee. When the knee is flexed and the medial and lateral ligaments are lax, the knee can easily be destabilized and twisted. The dancer must be properly trained to align the knee where it is squarely tracking over the foot as s/he proceeds into the *plié*. This is especially important in the takeoff and landing from a jump.

Many dancers (and athletes) have torn their cartilages and anterior cruciate ligaments (ACL) because of forceful rolling in/twisting of the knee. Great attention must be given to developing strength and control of the upper leg and hip along with the torso (center line of gravity) so that when the turnout is released in a *plié* position, it can maintain its alignment with the foot (figs. 3.10 and 3.11).

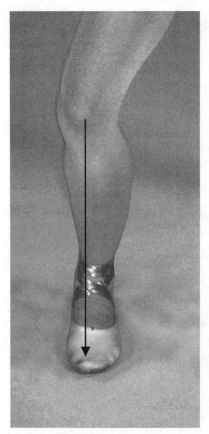 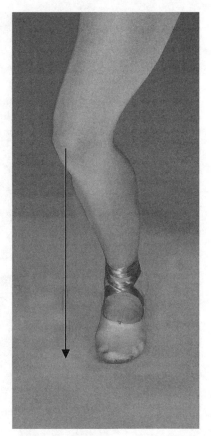

Fig. 3.10. Correct knee and foot
alignment.

Fig. 3.11. Incorrect knee and foot
alignment.

Teaching ballet has evolved greatly over the past few decades with our increased knowledge of kinesiology and development of sports medicine. Good teachers today use an anatomically based approach to ballet technique. This benefits students and professionals alike by anticipating and avoiding a lot of potential injuries that could end a dance career or aspirations for a career. It behooves every teacher to learn as much as possible about anatomy and how it pertains to what we do in the studio.

4

Music for Dance

Mastering the use of musical accompaniment can be the single most difficult aspect of teaching for most pedagogy students and young teachers.

There are two forms of accompaniment used for ballet class: recorded piano music on CD and live piano. Both forms have their advantages and disadvantages, and teachers usually prefer one over the other. However, having the sound and energy of a live piano establishes an atmosphere and a level of professionalism that recorded music cannot match.

Many beginning teachers at first are intimidated by working with pianists, just as there are some pianists who enjoy intimidating teachers a little—particularly if they sense that a teacher has little or no musical training. More often than not, the most experienced pianists are extremely patient and accommodating.

It is not imperative for a ballet teacher to have formal training in music, but it is reasonable to assume that any understanding of music fundamentals, its form and structure, will broaden and enrich one's teaching capabilities and effectiveness. Ballet is performed to music, and its kinesis and aesthetics work with many of the same components of music such as **meter**, **tempo**, **rhythm**, **accent**, **phrasing**, and **dynamics**.

Meter is the timing of music; it is the particular grouping together of beats. Tempo is the speed at which the music moves. Meter and tempo are an integral part of every ballet combination and exercise. It takes knowledge, experience, practice, and rhythmic sensitivity to know which meter and tempo will work best for each exercise. These elements, more than any other, will affect the dynamics and accurate technical execution of a ballet combination.

I often observe the frustration of many young teachers whose combinations do not work musically. They try to fix it—often unsuccessfully—by having the pianist adjust the tempo, when in fact it is the meter that doesn't work, or vice versa. I also watch students who eagerly and diligently try but are unsuccessful in applying corrections because the tempo or the meter is not conducive to the teacher's directive.

Not enough attention is paid to musical ear training during most of a young student's dance training. Many teachers who use recorded music by fine ballet pianists give little thought to choosing a track that has the best meter, tempo, and rhythm for the combinations and exercises. They simply count or pound out the beats in 8–count phrases and ignore the musical dynamics; they also don't take the time to stress to their students the importance of **listening** to the music and allowing it to inspire and create mood and imagery. As a result, many young dancers never develop a trained ear and have little understanding or feeling for music. Lack of musicality makes it impossible for a dancer to integrate movement and music on any sophisticated level.

Musicality in dance means that an integral relationship exists between music and movement. It can be simple and literal or, in the case of certain choreographic performances, sophisticated and abstract. By utilizing the subtlety of nuance in phrasing and counterpoint, this partnership offers many possibilities in movement qualities and textures. This applies not just to the creator (choreographer) but also to the dancer who executes and interprets the choreography.

Phrasing

We express ideas through our speech and writing by combining words, forming phrases, and creating sentences. Sentences are linked together into paragraphs, which collectively communicate a story, concept, or emotion. It can be literal or abstract. Music and dance do the same thing through sound and visual expressions.

A musical phrase is a self-contained musical sentence that is heard as a coherent and identifiable whole within the context of a composition.

Musical notes having various time values are grouped together with a given rhythmical pattern and are divided into sections called **bars** or **mea-**

sures. A measure or groups of measures create a musical phrase. A complete musical movement or composition features sections consisting of many connected phrases.

The defining characteristic of a phrase is the brief rest or sense of resolution at the end, which is called **cadence**. It is similar to the pauses we hear when someone speaks. Cadence enables us to hear phrasing easily.

When choreographing, we are creating **movement phrases**. Classical steps, stylized choreographic movements, and gestures are arranged with connecting steps to form combinations, or movement phrases that integrate in various ways with the music. And, as in music, many connecting phrases make up a complete dance.

A movement phrase, like a musical one, will have cadence—a pause, rest, or resolution—before beginning the next phrase. Movement phrases are not as easily identifiable as musical cadences because they are often visually quite subtle, with their execution dynamically internal. However, since they are integrated with the musical structure, they usually coincide with musical phrasing that is quite literal, particularly with studio teaching combinations.

Musicality

A choreographer chooses music that fits his concept or simply chooses to use a piece of music that inspires him to create movement that will interpret the score. The chosen music will often influence or even dictate how movements are constructed based on the various qualities and characteristics of the musical structure: rhythm, tempo, dynamics, mood, and melody. Linking and integrating the continuous musical and movement phrases establishes musicality in dance.

I can recall working in ABT with the renowned choreographer Antony Tudor. His musicality was impeccable. Each step and gesture of his choreography had meaning and was intricately tied to the music. He would often rehearse us by singing the counts or the names of the steps and directional changes, emphasizing phrasing and cadence through his voice. It was a powerful way to help the dancers bring choreography and music together.

Many choreographers work and count from the written musical score while they create a new work. However, most dancers have their own ambiguous and unorthodox way of counting music, often to the consternation of musicians. Trained dancers are expected to **hear** music; they are not handed a musical score from which to work. They must count and identify musical phrasing according to the way they hear it, or how the ballet master counts it, and how the movement phrases integrate with the music.

Meter and Rhythm

The beat is the feeling of pulse in the music. Musical notes and silent rests are each given a beat, or partial beat, with a specified time value and organized into bars. The total number of whole beats within the bar is called the meter. Beats are normally grouped into the following: 2's (duple meter—2/4), 3's (triple meter—3/4), or 4's (quadruple meter—4/4) with a certain beat being given a primary accent (usually the first beat) and sometimes secondary accents.

These bars, containing notes and rests with various durations, create a pattern that establishes a given rhythm. Dancers first listen for the pulses in music and assign a count to some or all of those beats. They then identify where the cadence is so that phrasing can be recognized. Accents are also identified as part of the dynamics; for example, a 3/4 waltz has the first beat accented—**1** 2 3/ **1** 2 3; in most mazurkas the end of the second beat has the accent: 1 **2** 3/ 1 **2** 3. Dancers also listen for the mood of the music through its feelings of texture along with dynamics: lyrical, percussive, syncopated, crescendo, rubato, etc.

Time signatures identify the meter. The time signature is stated at the beginning of the measure. Most recorded music for ballet class will specify the meter for each piece on the CD or its back cover and will often identify the rhythm, such as a waltz, polka, tango, *adage*, etc. The top number of a time signature denotes the number of beats in the measure. The bottom number denotes which note in each measure gets one full beat. The bottom number, however, is not something that we are immediately concerned with in working with class music. It does have relevance, though, once we become more sophisticated in using music.

Example: 3/4 = three beats in the measure; each quarter note gets one full beat.

4/4 = four beats in the measure; each quarter note gets one full beat.

6/8 = six beats in a measure; each eighth note gets one full beat.

The most common meters used in a ballet class are 2/4, 3/4, 4/4, and 6/8, simple time; 3/4 is also referred to as triple time or waltz time, and 4/4 is also called common time. The signatures 6/8, 9/8, and 12/8 are called compound time; their number of beats in the bar is divisible by three. Bars that have 5, 7, 11, or 13 beats, and therefore are not divisible by two or three, are called asymmetric time. It is uncommon to work with this type of music in ballet class, but it is common in modern dance classes and, of course, in performance music for choreography.

When requesting a duple meter, a teacher asks for a 2/4, but the pianist may in fact play a 4/4. It is difficult to distinguish the difference between these two time signatures without seeing the written music; it is possible in some compositions to count out two bars of 2/4 as a single bar of 4/4. So in most cases it is not going to matter whether a 2/4 or 4/4 is being played unless the timing and accent of an exercise or combination requires a strong 1–2/2–2/3–2/4–2.

Counting for Dance

Whenever possible, dancers try to group counts evenly together in phrases of 8 beats or 8 bars. Obviously, not all music is written in even 8's, but universally in ballet classes we devise combinations that count out in phrases of 8's and are grouped into even sections of 16, 32, or occasionally 64 counts. It is the responsibility of the ballet pianists to transpose written music to fit this structure or to play their own improvisation.

In order to keep track of how many groups of 8 are being counted while demonstrating a combination that has, for example, 32 counts, we would count 12345678/ 22345678 (=16), 32345678/ 42345678 (=32). This is an important method to remember because it is easy to lose track of what number group of 8's you are on while teaching a long adagio or grand allegro or planning your class combinations. I have watched student teachers get totally confused with counts when demonstrating a long combination because they didn't follow this method.

Generally, combinations are not designed with 12, 24, or 48 counts because it is musically contrary to traditional class structure. Therefore, recorded CD music is not done with that type of bar phrasing, nor do live ballet pianists transpose that way. Recorded CD tracks will sometimes have a **tag** of 8 or 16 counts at the end for the purpose of a finishing balance or *port de bras*. Teachers will often request this extra 8–bar or 16–bar extension of their accompanist.

Teachers/dancers assign a count to a step or group of steps. There can be a count for each beat or a fractional portion of the beats in a measure, or the entire measure can be regarded as one count, regardless of the actual number of beats denoted in the time signature. There really aren't any strict rules about counting in dance, and this is what causes some musicians to shake their heads in amazement. The tempo and type of music will determine how the dancer will count the measures. Pulse, tempo, accent/rhythm, and phrasing are the important determinations. Generally, dancers prefer to assign as many counts to movements and directional changes as possible without becoming cumbersome.

Here are some examples of how bars of music can be counted by a dancer/teacher:

One count per bar in a 3/4 waltz: 1 2 3/ 2 2 3/ 3 2 3/ 4 2 3 = 4 counts

One count per bar in a 2/4:   1 2/ 2 2/ 3 2/ 4 2 = 4 counts

One count per bar in a 4/4:   1 2 3 4/ 2 2 3 4/ 3 2 3 4/ 4 2 3 4 = 4 counts

Two counts per bar as in a 4/4:   1 2 3 4/ 2 2 3 4/ 3 2 3 4/ 4 2 3 4 = 8 counts

Or

1 and 2 and/ 3 and 4 and/ 5 and 6 and/ 7 and 8 and = 8 counts

One count for *each* beat (three counts) per bar as in a polonaise or slow mazurka:

1 2 3/ 2 2 3/ 3 2 3/ 4 2 3 = 12 counts [4–bar phrase]

In this last example, I have given one count to each beat in the bar, which seemingly would give us an uneven number of beats (12) in our phrasing according to our multiple 8–count rule. However, we often phrase according to bars rather than actual beats. In this case we have 12 beats in 4 bars. With this type of musical composition, we evenly group the number of bars—4, 8, 16—to establish cadence and phrasing. (Waltzes are also counted as one beat to the measure and grouped in multiples of 8.)

In ballet class we often use a polonaise or slow mazurka. They can be counted out in 4 bars of 3 beats per bar (actual counts), or we can combine 2 bars and give it a count of 6 beats per phrase. But regardless of how you group the counts, the number of bars must be even in your phrasing.

In a 6/8 meter, there are 6 beats in the bar. We usually don't give a dancer's count to each of the 6 beats or just 1 count for the entire bar. We usually give the bar a count of 2—on the first and fourth accented beats, and phrase it in 8's. Since a 6/8 meter has two accented beats in the bar, it can also be counted as a duple meter—2/4.

Now that we have seen examples of how dance counts can be assigned to bars of music, we must be careful not to disregard the beats within the bar that don't have a dance count. All of the beats along with every note and rest with varying time values must be acknowledged because they create the rhythm. And we must feel and hear the beats and rhythm as we dance and teach. So when we are counting, we simply give an **ee, and, uh** for the beats that do not get a numbered dancer's count.

Examples: Each number along with **ee-and-uh** has a pulse or beat. Try practicing this counting by tapping out all of the beats (**number ee-and-uh**) and saying the number out loud.

3/4 Waltz	1 count per bar	1 and-uh/ 2 and-uh/ 3 and-uh/ 4 and-uh
3/4 Polonaise	3 counts per bar	1–2–3/ 2–2–3/ 3–2–3/ 4–2–3
2/4	2 counts per bar	1–2/ 2–2/ 3–2/ 4–2
2/4	1 count per bar	1–and/ 2–and/ 3–and/ 4–and
4/4	4 counts per bar	1–2–3–4/ 2–2–3–4/ 3–2–3–4/ 4–2–3–4
4/4	2 counts per bar as if it were a 2/4	1–and 2–and/ /2–and 2–and/ 3–and 2–and/ 4–and 2–and
4/4	1 count per bar	1–ee–and–uh/ 2–ee–and–uh/ 3–ee–and–uh/ 4–ee–and–uh

This last one would only be counted this way if the tempo were quick. Otherwise, there would be too much time in between counts.

A beneficial exercise for understanding this is to practice with a ballet class music CD. Look to see what the time signature is for each track you listen to (number of beats in each bar) and tap out the pulses or beats while listening for accents, cadence, and phrasing. Then assign counts to the beats and bars in different ways using the above example as a guide. (The first beat in each bar is usually the strongest beat, called the primary accent).

In working with my student teachers, I require them to practice counting and phrasing by loudly verbalizing the **and-uh**. But I advise them to do it very softly or silently when they are teaching a class; otherwise, it quickly becomes annoying to everyone.

Learning how to demonstrate a combination using a clearly recognizable duple or triple meter is an important teaching quality. While you are demonstrating, think of the music you have chosen or expect your accompanist to play (rhythm and phrasing) and integrate it into the rhythm and cadence of your voice. It will help your students and your accompanist.

Working with an Accompanist

Too often, much of the live music that is played for ballet class is hackneyed and uninspiring and does little more than establish a supporting beat. But a seasoned accompanist who is familiar with ballet and the dynamics of movement will choose appropriate music that will support the dancer's execution of a combination. The right choice of music along with the sensitivity of the pianist can enhance an exercise and give an added dimension to your entire class.

Pianists possess varying degrees of ability, sensitivity, and commitment to their accompanying. Some are extremely accommodating while others can be quite difficult. The ideal pianist is one who collaborates, pays attention, and understands the dynamics of movement and the art of ballet. The most important elements of his/her playing are a steady tempo and the ability to change that tempo instantly at the teacher's cue.

The pianist's responsibility is not only to support the ballet combinations but also to inspire the dancers with his/her music. An experienced accompanist who understands ballet is an invaluable part of the teaching process. A poor pianist will diminish or even ruin an otherwise well structured class.

The following points can be valuable when working with a pianist:

1. If this is your first time working together, introduce yourself and establish a personal connection. After all, the two of you will be communicating with each other throughout the entire class. Address your accompanist by his/her name.

2. Do not allow a pianist to intimidate you. S/he is there for you, not vice versa. You are not expected to be a musician. But it is the pianist's job to know about ballet movement and instruction and how to follow and accompany it.

3. Let your pianist know if there are certain types of music you prefer or do not want played. Some pianists like to improvise or play their own compositions, show tunes, or other nontraditional music.

4. Establish how you will communicate tempo and meter during the class. There are several ways of doing this: (a) announce which meter you want (specifically, or just say duple or triple meter, or a waltz, gallop, etc.), and briefly count or beat out the tempo, (b) hum or sing a few improvised bars of your desired meter, tempo, and rhythm directly to your pianist (I have seen well-known teachers do this; it is quick and simple, so don't be afraid to sing), and (c) communicate the tempo and meter through the rhythm and cadence of your voice as you demonstrate and count out the exercise.

   Create music in your mind while you demonstrate. For the sake of pacing, when communicating the tempo and meter through the rhythm and cadence of your voice, set your tempo at the beginning of the combination so that you establish it with your pianist, and then, if it is a long combination, you can go through the remaining parts a little more quickly. It is a good idea at the end of the demonstration to reestablish the desired tempo. Communicate to your accompanist before class, if you have never worked together, how you are setting tempo. It is very frustrating for the accompanist (and students) when a teacher demonstrates without communicating a meter or setting a tempo.

5. Give as much information as you can to your accompanist before and/or during your demonstration. Let her/him know that you want a specific type of music, such as mazurka instead of a waltz or a tango instead of an *adage*. Don't expect your accompanist to produce a specific piece instantly, especially if s/he must look for it in a binder of sheet music. The more time your pianist has to prepare for the exercise or combination, the better chance you have of getting what you want musically, and you will be able to maintain a steadier teaching pace.

6. Many pianists do not use sheet music; they play off the top of their head. There are some excellent nationally known accompanists who are able to do this well, but I think they are few and far between. Pianists who do not bring sheet music with them are often lazy and are limited in what they can play. If you find that this is the case with your accompanist, insist that s/he bring a diverse repertoire of sheet music to class.

7. Treat your accompanist collaboratively and with respect. Of course, this must be reciprocal. If you need to scold or correct something really negative about your accompanist's playing, it is best if you walk over to the piano to speak privately. Do not address her/him from across the room in front of the students.

Discuss with your accompanist what you liked, what worked best, and what didn't work well. If there is a piece of music that you particularly liked or disliked, let her/him know right then and there so s/he can make a note of it. The majority of accompanists want to please and be collaborative, but I have found through experience that it is the teacher who is expected to initiate the conversation.

✿

It is helpful to be able to communicate to your pianist using musical terms and movement metaphors that describe the feel or dynamics of a combination instead of just saying, "slower," "faster," "play something else," etc.

Tempo markings describe the general rate of speed, and they are usually indicated by Italian terms. Exact tempo is set according to a predetermined range on the metronome. (A metronome is a device that ticks a given number of times per minute.) Listening to classical music is a good way to familiarize yourself with tempo.

Tempo in ballet is determined according to the ability to perform certain steps within a range of speeds.

The following tempo and dynamics terms can be used loosely as a reference point between you and your pianist.

Tempo

Largo (LARH-goh)	Very slow and broad
Lento (LEN-toh)	Slow
Adagio (ah-DAH-joh)	Slow, between largo and andante
Andante (ahn-DAHN-teh)	Moderate graceful tempo; walking speed.
Moderato (moh-deh-RAH-toh)	Moderate tempo
Allegro (ahl-LAY-groh)	Fast
Allegretto (ahl-leh-GRET-toh)	Slightly slower than allegro
Vivace (vee-VAH-cheh)	Lively
Presto (PRES-toh)	Very fast

Dynamics consist of degrees of loudness and softness in the music. Dance dynamics are expressed through the degree of energy or force used to execute and project a movement.

Legato (leh-GAH-toh)	Smooth, without strong accents
Staccato (stahk-KAH-toh)	Sharp, stabbing
Pizzicato (peed-zee-KAH-toh)	Plucking, to pluck a string

Dynamic metaphors used in dance movement can also be helpful in communicating with your accompanist: *percussive, lyrical, suspension, bouncing, driving, gliding, darting,* etc. If your pianist is experienced in ballet accompaniment, s/he will tune into the movement dynamics and know which music to choose.

To thoroughly articulate instructions to the pianist is a must. But when there is no live accompaniment, the teacher must choose music from compact discs that will best support each exercise and combination regarding tempo, meter, rhythm, and dynamic quality.

If you are teaching with CDs:

1. Buy CDs that give you the meter for each track; if it also describes the rhythm, this is even better.

2. Know your music. Become familiar with the tracks in terms of tempo, meter, and rhythm. Be aware that tracks that are designated for the barre work and those for the center floor are interchangeable. *Plié* music can also be used as an *adage*, or the *petit battement* track might be used instead for small jumps or *chaîné* turns.

3. Know what meter and tempo you need for each exercise and combination as you plan your class and, ideally, which piece of music you will use. Sequentially, jot down the meters, CD title, and track numbers in such a way that you can glance at them easily.

4. Try to use no more than two or three CDs for your class. It will be less time-consuming and cumbersome.

5. If using a multiple CD changer, load the CDs chronologically in the tray, and lay out the CD cover or insert with the track and meter information in the same order as the CD tray number for easy referral.

6. A lot of time is wasted by fiddling with CDs and sound equipment, which can negatively affect the pacing of your class and allow children to become distracted. Using a remote control for the CD player will save time.

5

The Teaching and Learning Process

Class Levels

Dance schools usually divide students into four categories based on age: primary or predance (below the age of 6), preadolescent (ages 6–10), early adolescent (ages 11–15), and late adolescent through adult (ages 16 and up). Primary and preadolescent levels make up a lower school or division, and the adolescent and adult levels constitute an upper division.

Guiding and mentoring students through the training process is different at each of these levels because of the intellectual and psychological/emotional development of each age group. It is rare that a teacher is equally effective and comfortable in teaching all levels. More often than not, teachers are more comfortable and better suited for teaching in just one division—upper or lower school. I know teachers who only teach upper intermediate through professional levels and who would never take on a children's class, and conversely, there are those who teach children who would never consider teaching a professional level class.

Not all schools have the resources or enrollments to separate their intensive (preprofessional) students from their recreational students. This creates a challenge for teachers because the extent of mentoring and performance expectations is dissimilar between these two groups, giving a different emphasis to the student/teacher relationship.

Teaching in a local dance studio or community center can have a much different set of expectations for both the teacher and the student. Most students attend primarily for the recreational enjoyment of dancing and without any ambitions for a career in the art. The benchmarks and timelines for progress will be different and lower than those in a preprofessional career program; therefore, this should be reflected in whatever expectations a teacher has for the overall class.

But this is not to say that there should be any diminution of the quality of training and conveyed artistic values. There are many talented youngsters who are potentially fine dancers attending local dance studios, and a strong technical foundation will help ensure their success if and when they progress into a preprofessional training program.

We teach and our students learn via the cognitive and kinesthetic processes. Students cognize and process information visually through our demonstrations of steps and spatial relationships, and they hear through our verbal instruction, which often includes imagery and musical rhythm. Kinesthetic learning is experiential—knowing how a movement feels by doing it. Hence serious dance students take daily classes and practice the same steps over and over.

As with all forms of concert dance, ballet is taught primarily through group learning rather than in private sessions. This presents an added challenge to any teacher as s/he offers general corrections throughout a class, because each student has his/her own system of cognitive and kinesthetic learning. Personal corrections are given as well, but the same correction given to two students may be effective for one but not for the other. It is, therefore, up to the teacher to ascertain or intuit how each student learns effectively.

The Student/Teacher Relationship

Perfecting technique is unquestionably necessary in order to become a professional dancer and artist. More and more of today's young dancers exhibit highly refined technique and are capable of executing very difficult steps. But technique is only half of the whole; it is the means by which dancers attain and fully express their artistry. Too often we see young dancers perform classical variations, especially in national competitions, where a fine line separates their performances between that of a circus act and the high art of classical ballet. So, as teachers, we must do more than just teach steps.

When I first began to teach, my goals were simply to design a class and present it clearly. If the class went smoothly, I declared it a success. Most of my attention was focused on my own pedagogical skills. As I became more adept and comfortable with teaching, I was able to concentrate more on understanding the relationship that exists between the student and teacher and how the process of teaching and learning develops and matures.

Developing a relationship with students, especially in a preprofessional environment, is the first step to mastering the training process. It is an equal partnership in which the teacher and student each have a designated responsibility to recognize and fulfill.

With preprofessional and recreational students alike, teachers impart not only the technical knowledge of ballet but also its artistic sensibilities, and they facilitate the students' ability to understand and assimilate them. We foster the desire, love, and enthusiasm for the art of ballet and give positive reinforcement for progress made and encouragement for what yet needs to be mastered. We expose our students to what is refined and tasteful in artistic expression and guide them to emulate these qualities. We accomplish all of this by instilling self-discipline, along with the ability to concentrate, and we mentor them as they develop individual determination and a dedicated professional work ethic.

Students are expected to bring to the teacher a willingness to put forth maximum effort, including consistency in attendance, and to accept the teacher and what is taught unhesitatingly. Adhering to traditional etiquette of the ballet studio is imperative. It involves arriving on time, being properly dressed, following directions, accepting criticism, and being attentive and respectful toward the teacher. When a student begins to argue, misbehave, and resist corrections, it is time for him/her to seek out another teacher, because without complete trust and respect, the training development is breached.

The teacher is the source of artistic and technical knowledge, and s/he imparts, facilitates, and mentors. It is the student, as the recipient and beneficiary of this knowledge, who is ultimately responsible for his/her own development. However, this is not always evident to young dancers, who may think that they need only attend class regularly and coast along on automatic pilot in order to progress. Martha Graham wrote, "Dancers keep looking for the perfect teacher without realizing that it's all there within themselves. They have to be responsible for themselves. You teach yourself;

the teacher is the guide. If you do not hear the advice, corrections, and words of your guide, it makes no difference how great the teacher. You will never dance."

∽

Training to be a dancer is a slow, laborious process that takes a great deal of patience and consistent commitment. After a certain amount of progress is gained, a plateau is reached, and the student may remain there for some time before s/he or the teacher sees another surge of progress. This is natural, and everyone experiences it. Nevertheless, it can be frustrating and discouraging. At these times, encouraging and supportive words from the teacher are called for, along with explaining how these plateaus are part of being a dancer.

Throughout the years of training before the advanced levels are reached, many young students (and sometimes parents) have difficulty realizing that specific corrections (individual or general) must be applied before more advanced directives or corrections can be given. It is an evolving process of layering adjustments and corrections with an ever-increasing level of technical and artistic sophistication. Each student has his/her individual learning curve. The curve is affected by talent and ability, desire and determination—sometimes overcoming physical disadvantages—and it requires his/her own time frame to assimilate and apply the reinforced corrections of the teacher.

When students understand and have correctly applied what is taught, they are ready to be given more. Of course, a dancer who has the facility to immediately comprehend and apply what is taught is the ideal student. The faster a student can learn, the more information a teacher can give. This defines much of the teacher-student partnership in the teaching-learning process. We have an obligation to those students who learn quickly, to teach them without delay as much as they can absorb and apply. (Less devoted or talented students sometimes wrongly interpret this as favoritism.)

We also live in a society that breeds expectations of instant gratification. Many students fantasize about a professional career in dance, but only a small percentage will have the mettle to succeed. Those who are lazy, uncommitted, or lacking in the talent or facility to dance will eventually become discouraged and quit. And sometimes these students blame the teacher or the school rather than themselves. A couple of the universal criticisms that you may eventually be subjected to are "My teacher gives most of his/her attention to a few favorite students" and "My teacher never pays attention or gives corrections to me." Don't get thrown when you hear this for the first or second time—it is a common remark. Taking the focus off one's shortcomings and redirecting it at someone else is a natural human characteristic, and it can happen with any student.

I regularly share the following advice with my students:

1. Be focused, work very hard and with consistency, and be patient with yourself. There is no instant gratification in the art of ballet.

2. Respect your teachers and listen carefully to what they say, even when it is not personally directed at you.

3. Don't be critical or envious of other dancers. We have different bodies (instruments) with individual strengths and weaknesses. Perfect your own strengths and improve your own weaknesses.

4. Competition in class is healthy. If there is a lack of competition, compete with yourself! Try to be a better dancer today than you were yesterday.

Establishing Good Technical Habits

As toddlers, we learn to walk by carefully and consciously placing one foot in front of the other while precariously balancing our torso on the top of our legs. After some falls and perhaps a few tears, we develop the muscular coordination to stand upright and walk balanced on both legs. Eventually, we learn to walk and run without having to consciously send commands to our limbs to put one leg forward and then the other and so on. We learn to ride a bicycle in the same manner by balancing the weight of our torso while coordinating pedaling and steering. With time and repetitive practice, riding becomes second nature. The same process happens in ballet training but on a much more complex and sophisticated level.

One of the most operative words in ballet training is *repetition*. By repeating a step or movement over and over, a habit pattern is established in the brain, sort of like pressing grooves in a vinyl recording—or, in today's technical parlance, burning a CD—but doing it through the brain cells. When the brain, via the central and peripheral nervous systems, directs the body to do a certain movement, it happens automatically in the exact way it was learned and established as a physical movement pattern through repetition. For example, let us look at the complicated execution of a *pirouette:* the *relevé* through the supporting leg, the position of the working leg and foot in *retiré,* the directional pattern of the arms, the spotting of the head, and the rotation of the torso all happen as sequentially smooth, coordinated movements without us consciously thinking about each relative part. This is the unconscious or automatic synapse between the mind and the body, referred to as *muscle memory* or *movement habit.*

Many professional dancers say that we take class every day to perfect our technique so we can go onstage and forget about technique and concentrate on artistic expression and interpretation. But this is possible to do only after years of practice, establishing the correct muscle memory.

Dancers develop a highly complex system of movement habits. Once a bad habit has been established, it can be hard to undo. The brain and muscles do not initially know whether the execution of a step is technically correct or not. We condition our brain to think a step is being done correctly based on the habitual physical sensations of its muscular execution through repetition.

This is why it is so important to establish correct technique and placement at the outset. Undoing a bad habit and relearning the same movement correctly requires much more effort on the part of the teacher and student.

Many students are initially reluctant to apply certain corrections that require moving differently because the new way feels uncomfortable and foreign, while the old way feels comfortable. This is where the element of trust between teacher and student is paramount. It also takes constant diligence and perseverance to break bad habits and establish correct technique.

Many excellent teachers find themselves spending as much time undoing bad training as they do teaching initial good habits!

6

Teaching Your Class

Historically, many if not most ballet teachers have believed that students can and should learn ballet by rote—learning through mechanical, unthinking repetition. Classical ballet positions and movements are repeated over and over with little or no mindfulness of why a particular exercise is done and with little or no understanding of anatomy and the physics of movement. Giving the sequence of a class over and over and training strictly by rote minimally benefits only the naturally gifted students. Most dancers who learn to dance this way can often look static and posed and rarely express a true and authentic feeling for movement.

Repetition is undoubtedly essential in all ballet training, but it should be done with full comprehension. Students also have a much better chance to develop into good technicians and artists when they learn from teachers who are knowledgeable of anatomy and the kinesthetic and artistic elements of ballet movement and who are musical enough to know how to use tempo, meter, and rhythm. These teachers know the importance of how connecting steps along with the use of dynamics (force and time) turns ballet exercises into artistic movement. Fortunately, the teaching profession has evolved over the past few decades, and a far greater number of teachers reflect a more comprehending and analytical approach to teaching and explaining technique.

Each year one of the first things I would explain to my new class of university pedagogy students, who exhibited varying degrees of self-confidence and nervousness, is that when you walk into a ballet studio to teach, you are in an authoritative position. Your students rely on your expertise and guidance, and they expect you to radiate a demeanor of authority. They want you to nurture and inspire them.

Therefore, learn to take control of the room from the moment you walk in. Regardless of how nervous or unsure you might feel at first, it is essential that you portray a demeanor of self-confidence and experienced ability. If necessary, rely for a while on the old maxim "Fake it 'til you make it." This does not mean, however, that you should put on a phony façade and behave in an insincere way. Demonstrating self-confidence and authority though being a little unsure, even feeling some nervous butterflies in the stomach, does not signify insincerity. It is in some ways much like getting used to public speaking. So be patient, as these teaching qualities will develop naturally over time through experience.

Sincerity in your teaching and the rapport that you develop with each student are the building blocks of trust that must exist within the foundation of every student's training. Students, especially children, have an uncanny ability to sense when a teacher is not being sincere. And if that should happen, you risk losing their respect and possibly even control of your class.

Your teaching manner should also reflect the expectations you have for your students. Expectations should be realistic and correspond to the types of students and to the teaching setting, i.e., professional, preprofessional, local suburban studio, community center or YMCA, etc. Often a teacher will be working in multiple settings that will require a change in mind-set while traveling from one studio to the next. It is not always easy to change gears, and it takes a concerted effort to go off to a class of junior high school students who dance once or twice a week for the enjoyment of it after you have just come from a pre-professional school where the students have professional aspirations.

Whatever the teaching setting, you must always teach with integrity and professionalism. Always try to teach by invitation, not by intimidation. And never, ever demean your students! That type of teaching approach is counterproductive.

Another part of every student's training foundation is how to conduct himself or herself in the studio. Students should be instructed to adhere to a proper code of behavior as dictated by centuries-old tradition and etiquette in classical ballet. By doing so, you will find it easier to maintain authority and control of your class.

The following are a few of the traditional rubrics for students that I recommend be part of your school's culture. It should be included in the class schedule or studio handbook and displayed prominently in the school:

1. Arrive on time and remain for the whole class unless permission has been given to leave early.

2. Always acknowledge and thank your teacher when leaving early by permission.

3. Let your teacher know before class if you have an injury or physical issues.

4. Never leave the studio during class without permission.

5. Be properly dressed—which does not mean in whatever happens to be today's fashion trend. Choose attire that will enable your teacher to see your body properly. Girls should have their hair securely up.

6. Stand up when your teacher enters the studio to begin class.

7. Never chit-chat during class. Request to be recognized before speaking to your teacher.

8. Always be attentive when your teacher is speaking.

9. Never sit down, especially when your teacher is demonstrating.

10. Never turn your back to your teacher when he/she is speaking or demonstrating.

11. Keep an open and receptive body posture. Avoid stances such as hands on the hips, arms folded across the chest, etc.

12. Applaud your teacher at the end of class as a sign of respect and gratitude, and acknowledge the pianist. It is also common practice for each student to approach the teacher to personally thank him/her along with a handshake, bow, or curtsy.

Teaching ballet or any concert dance form requires the coordination and inclusion of various pedagogical skills:

1. Knowledge and application of posture and placement and the directional lines of the body.

2. Teaching and demonstrating.

3. Mirroring.

4. Cueing and counting.

5. Correcting.

6. Pacing.

7. Teaching demeanor and energy level.

8. Use of the voice.

9. Effective use of music.

10. Teaching through touch.

11. Teaching through imagery.

The objectives for your class have been set, and the lesson plan has been structured with a logical sequence. Now we turn to the skill of teaching it.

Directions of the Body in Presenting and Viewing Ballet

As students come away from the barre for center floor exercises, close attention should be paid to the angle and line of each position and movement as it is viewed from the front. Ballet is traditionally performed on a proscenium theater stage as opposed to a thrust or horseshoe stage, or theatre-in-the-round, and choreography is crafted accordingly. The lines and angles of *croisé, ouvert, de coté, écarté, en face*, etc., must be done correctly and with precision; otherwise, it will change the look of the position or movement, and the choreography. To assist us in this we have the points of the dancer's square. There are eight points that theoretically correspond to, but should not be confused with, the directions of the stage or studio from center stage. These numbered points refer to each dancer's individual directional square. Traditional stage directions are downstage and upstage, stage right and left,

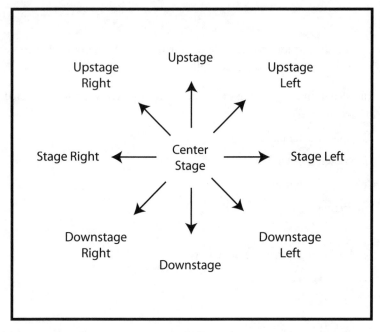

Diagram 6.1. Stage directions.

downstage right and left, and upstage right and left (diagram 6.1). There is a common misconception among some teachers that the points of the dancer's square refer to the corners, front, back, and side walls of the studio, regardless of where one is positioned in the room or onstage.

The way to learn these points of direction is to imagine standing in the center of your own personal square. (Drawing a chalk square of equal dimensions around each of your beginner students and numbering each point is an effective way to teach this.) Two directional numbering systems are used. Maestro Cecchetti numbers the points beginning with the downstage right corner of his square and proceeding counterclockwise (diagram 6.2). Madame Vaganova numbers her square beginning with downstage center and proceeding clockwise (diagram 6.3). I have found the use of the Cecchetti square to be more prevalent in the United States and Great Britain, perhaps because of Cecchetti's influence on the Ballets Russes and the Royal Ballet, and so I will use that numbering system in the following examples.

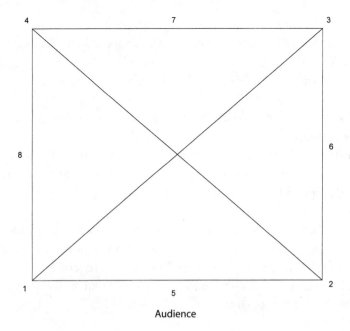

Diagram 6.2. Cecchetti points of the square.

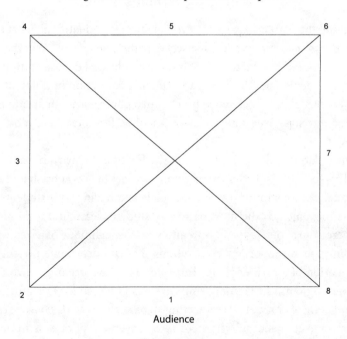

Diagram 6.3. Vaganova's points of the square.

The basic positions of the body along with the *arabesques* are accurately positioned according to the points of the dancer's individual square as viewed from the front (audience). As with *tendu croisé devant* facing point 2, the torso and working leg are square to point 2, and the head/*épaulement* is directed to point 5 (*en face*). In *écarté* facing point 1, the torso is square to point 1, and the working leg and head are directed to point 2. *Arabesque de côté* (sideways/profile), the torso and head are directed to point 6, and the working leg is extended to point 8, or vice versa. If the torso, head, or working leg is facing or pointed somewhere in between two fixed points, the classical shape and line of the position as viewed from the front are altered and compromised.

One of the more consistent mistakes I see is when a student prepares for a *pirouette* in *croisé* fourth position and squares off to the downstage corner of the studio instead of corner 1 or 2 of his/her own square. As a result, the upstage half of the torso and shoulder is usually obscured, and the position looks more profile than *croisé*.

Teaching and Demonstrating

Explaining the correct way to perform a ballet step, identifying what a student is doing incorrectly, and concisely explaining how to correct the error are the essence of good teaching. It is done by physical demonstration and/ or verbal articulation. The ability to explain a correction in different ways using various physical reference points, metaphors, and visualizations is a skill that develops over many years of teaching. It is a teacher's most valuable asset.

Your syllabus and lesson plan form the foundation for your class structure. This foundation is the starting point from which you teach and communicate. Demonstrating a step completely and having your students imitate the movement is the most basic way students learn, but it should not end there. You should explain how and why the technique of a step works, including the all-important preparations that can determine the successful execution of a turn or jump. This often requires breaking down a step and pointing out how learning simpler steps prepared for this more difficult and complex one. How connecting steps such as *pas de bourrée, coupe,* and *précipité* connect multiple steps into movement phrases is important to explain and incorporate into your teaching as students become more advanced. (Refer to the phrasing section in chapter 4.) Students should be required to learn the French ballet vocabulary. In children's classes, many teachers require their students to know the meaning and correct spelling of all the French ballet steps and terms by keeping a vocabulary notebook.

Only the most experienced teachers have the ability to teach a good solid class off the top of their head, and even then it can be a hit-or-miss event. So be prepared before you walk into your class. Know your lesson plan; either have it memorized or have abbreviated notes where, at a glance, you will be able to recall any combination. Few things are more irritating for students than having to stand around waiting while their teacher deciphers his/her notes or designs an impromptu exercise. If you find that notes are needed, try to quickly glance at and review the next exercise while your students are finishing the current exercise; in that way you will avoid a long pause between exercises. This will require some good abbreviated notation.

Memorize your counts and know the tempo and meter for each combination. As you demonstrate try to communicate the tempo and meter through the rhythmical accent and cadence of your voice. This is helpful not only to your students for when they do hear the music but also for your pianist. Make sure that combinations phrase evenly in 8, 16, or 32 measures. Unless you are working with a pianist, have your music laid out and ready to go. By that I mean have your CDs out of their cases and lined up or inserted in the player in proper order if you are using a multi-changer player. (Using a remote control is particularly helpful.) Make a list of which CD and track number you are using for each exercise, or write it alongside your class notation. If you can't recall a specific meter or tempo before you begin demonstrating, quickly play a few measures of the CD track. If necessary, demonstrate with the music, but keep in mind that doing so usually eats up more time. It is important to get through your demonstrations and directives as quickly and as thoroughly as possible.

In order not to run out of time, whenever I demonstrate an exercise that has a slow to moderate tempo, I start and finish the demonstration with the correct tempo, but I will speed up the middle parts a little, and my students (and pianist) have no difficulty clueing into the correct tempo.

Be careful not to overwhelm your students with too much information; allow them time to assimilate incrementally what they are given. Don't try to teach all the refinements of a new step at once. Many new teachers in their eagerness to share their knowledge often wind up giving a mini lecture about each ballet exercise before and after their students execute it. Ballet technique is complicated, and it takes a long time to understand all of its complexities. Therefore, know what you want to say about a step or exercise and try to explain succinctly what you expect to see.

Keep your demonstrations, especially at the barre, as simple and straightforward as possible. Unless the students already know the combination from a previous class, their minds will be concentrated on memorizing the sequence. Give them time to absorb the pattern of movement before interjecting technical and musical directives. Once your students have the exercise memorized, you can give them more information. This is why I often repeat combinations from class to class or teach the same class for a set period of time. Students are then able to really concentrate on the technique and performance of the exercise, and they have minimal mental energy concentrated on remembering sequence.

Your demonstrations and explanations concerning the correct execution of a step or combination should always be done clearly, thoroughly, and above all, briefly. It is valuable to point out specific goals of technique before the students do it, but not always. It is often better to watch your students do the exercise first so you can identify the pertinent technical, musical, and artistic points that need to be addressed. It is irrelevant and a waste of time to remind your students how to do something right when they are already doing it correctly. Look for and address what is immediately relevant. Also, giving short general and specific corrections while students are dancing trains them to listen and immediately process the correction and apply it kinetically.

Teachers have a tendency to demonstrate all the time on the same side, usually with the left hand on the barre and with the right working side in center. This is not a good habit, as it results in an imbalance with one side of the body becoming much stronger than the other. Students may experience this, too, if they are following you in the demonstration. So alternate sides when you demonstrate (your body will be grateful). In addition, have your students alternate the beginning side of the barre: for example, begin all exercises with the left hand on the barre for one week and change to the right hand the following week. (This is done in the Cecchetti Method.) Center floor combinations can also begin with alternating sides.

Demonstrating over many years can be very hard, even destructive, on a teacher's body, especially if one is muscularly cold before beginning class. Unfortunately, the ill effects of this do not manifest until years later. Therefore, take the time to warm up before teaching and don't demonstrate every exercise full-out. This is easier to do, of course, with advanced/intermediate and advanced classes; children and beginner levels require clearer and more fully demonstrated teaching. Having advanced students come into these classes as demonstrators can be of great help in this area.

Don't rush through the class in order to complete your lesson plan. Doing so will not accomplish your teaching objectives in the long run. One of the principal goals of a ballet dancer is to perfect technique while building strength and flexibility. Therefore, allocate enough time to methodically take him/her through the execution of a step.

The most valuable and desirable qualities that a director or choreographer looks for in a dancer are cleanliness and precision in technique and an unmannered simplicity of style, thereby allowing the specific style of their choreography to come through. With that in mind, avoid stylistic flourishes and affectations when you are teaching and demonstrating, and discourage these things if your students incorporate them on their own into their dancing.

There are various essential skills that constitute the teaching process and automatically, for the most part, become incorporated into your delivery and demonstration. We don't often consciously think about these individual parts that make up the whole, but in order to evaluate and critique our own teaching and that of others we need to define and understand what they are and how they fit into our overall teaching. These skills are mirroring, cueing and counting, teaching demeanor and energy level, giving corrections that include the use of imagery and touch, using music effectively, and modulating your voice.

Mirroring

Mirroring is an important skill to develop immediately. It is the method of facing your students while demonstrating and using the opposite side of your body from that of your students. It precludes the necessity of turning your back to your dancers and speaking away from them rather than toward them. This is particularly important when teaching children and beginners because you need to watch them to see that they are correctly following your demonstrations. Plus, it is always more effective to teach face-to-face and eye-to-eye.

Developing and perfecting the skill of mirroring takes practice and concentrated effort. It is one more skill layered over those of remembering the exercise sequence and counting in correct tempo and meter. It requires you to refer to your students' right working side while your working side is left, and vice versa. It can be confusing in the beginning for new teachers, but it is an important teaching tool for demonstrating center work, particularly barre work for children and adult beginners.

When demonstrating barre work to children and beginners, place a portable demonstration barre at either end of the studio so that you can be seen easily and can demonstrate the next exercise without having to walk to the opposite end of the studio. It is best, but not always possible, to have your students face you with the same hand on the barre. Place your opposite hand on the barre from that of the students while facing them so that your working side arm and leg mirror their working side. Become accustomed to saying **right** when you are demonstrating with the left side and **left** when you are demonstrating right. Older adolescents and adults will sometimes not catch on that you are mirroring and will need to be told to use the opposite side. But children are especially receptive to following a mirror image.

Demonstrating center floor is more complicated when *adage*, turn, and jump combinations become more advanced. Classical positions of the body and certain movements that have changes of direction (e.g., facing different points of the square and promenades) can be easier for students to learn following the teacher from behind rather than mirroring. Once your students have learned the combination sequence, you should then face them to give technical directives and corrections and reintroduce the mirroring tool when appropriate. Keep in mind, however, that when you demonstrate with your back to the students, you will be speaking away from them and thus will need to increase the volume of your voice. Also, if you are not in front of a full-length mirror, they will not be able to see the reflection of your front.

Many schools allow students to face full-length mirrors during center floor work. This can make demonstrating with your back to them easier because your students can also see your front via the mirror reflection. But the mirror is a tool that dancers need to be taught how to use. It is for visually analyzing a correction that cannot be easily felt and for checking the line and shape of a position. Kinetically **feeling** correct positions, *épaulement,* and movement dynamics is more important than just visually validating their accuracy in the mirror.

Cueing and Counting

Cueing is the prompt you call out to students that helps them with counts, the sequence of a combination, or technical directives and corrections. Just as teachers have to learn to develop exercises in eight-count phrases, students must learn to hear musical phrasing and count in multiples of eight. Guiding them in their counts is a form of cueing. Cueing is also helpful and necessary when there is an exercise or sequence of longer or more complicated combinations and when corrections need to be given during the performance of a combination. Even the simplest exercises require you to cue when teaching children, adult beginners, and some intermediate levels.

Effective cueing is a matter of timing. If it pertains to sequencing or directives, it must be anticipated so it is communicated to the students right before it is relevant but with enough time for them to mentally register it and apply the action. It is a very fast process. To do this well, the teacher must watch how the student performs in the moment while simultaneously foreseeing difficulties or errors and quickly reacting with a concise and articulate comment. As with all of the other teaching skills, this takes practice.

Seeing common technical faults and correcting by cueing students as they dance is often an efficient way of teaching, as you do not have to stop the class, correct, and begin again. This avoids any disruption in your pacing and energy level. Some students have difficulty hearing and applying a cueing directive from their teacher because they are unable to perform a movement and process a directive simultaneously. But with time, most students gain the ability to do it.

Counting beats is an integral part of demonstrating and cueing. The following is a brief recap of essential points that will assist you in counting and phrasing. Chapter 4 explains counting in much greater detail.

The manner in which you count and use your voice can establish a clearly defined phrasing in your demonstrations. Therefore, it is important to practice incorporating rhythm and cadence while demonstrating so that you clearly communicate a duple or triple meter. With time and practice working on musical accents, your voice should be able to make a distinction between a waltz and a mazurka, a polka and a gallop, a march and a tango, etc.

When you are constructing your lesson plan, be diligent about building combinations that have even phrasing. Traditionally, ballet combinations and the accompanying music are structured in even multiples of 8 counts: 8, 16, and 32. As you are demonstrating, it is important to keep track of how many phrases of 8's have been counted. An uneven number will leave you and your students hanging musically.

Also while demonstrating, it will help you to stay in your selected meter if you count 1 and/ 2 and/ 3 and/ 4 and when you are using a duple meter. In a 3/4 waltz meter, it will be 1 and-uh/ 2 and-uh/ 3 and-uh/ 4 and-uh. The **and** plus **uh** represent the other two beats in the musical measure. Once you are comfortable with counting this way, try to do the **and** plus **and-uh** silently, as it gets tiresome for everyone listening to these word beats with every combination.

Many of the music CDs for ballet have the meters listed on the insert and will often identify selections as a waltz, a march, etc. These can be used as good learning tools if you are not trained in music.

Giving Corrections

Our bodies are complicated mechanisms, being our trained instruments for the highly sophisticated technique of classical ballet. Technical perfection in ballet is elusive: it is there one day and absent the next. Therefore, perfecting and sustaining one's technique takes diligence and patience.

Corrections can be given verbally as well as visually through demonstration. Young teachers who are accomplished in their own dancing are more apt to show their students the correction because it's easier for them than finding the right words to articulate it. The danger with this and all demonstrations is that you might show a step incorrectly or in a sloppy manner, especially to students who predominantly learn visually, including children. As we become older and more experienced in teaching, we develop our individual lexicon of phrases and words for correcting technical errors and for explaining more abstract things, such as movement dynamics and interpretation. Our ability to correct effectively will continue to develop and refine with consistent teaching experience. Strive to be brief and comprehensive. Give as much information as needed in as few words as possible.

Elements for good teaching are a thorough understanding of classical technique and a keen **eye** that can quickly and distinctly identify technical and stylistic problems. These enable the teacher to anticipate and address common faults relating to each step while cueing and correcting students as they perform them.

Some corrections are straightforward: point the foot, straighten the knee, square off the back, pull up the abdominals, etc. Visual images can be quite simple and literal, which they should be when you are teaching children who have not yet matured enough to understand symbolic or abstract concepts. Nonfigurative corrections are those that use metaphors and physical reference points that create abstract visual images of how the implementation of a movement should look and/or feel. An example of this would be imagining simultaneous opaque ribbons or streams of energy in a *pirouette* where one directional force pushes downward into the floor in the *relevé* while the other revolving force spirals in opposition upward. These types of images and directives can be quite effective, but they are not always interpreted the same way by each student. Therefore, a teacher will find it necessary to have numerous ways of giving the same correction to different students.

When you are giving a correction or technical explanation, allow students to apply it immediately by repeating either the position or step or the entire combination. Dancers learn by applying what is taught and physically experiencing the feeling of doing a movement in a new or modified and corrected way. So give them that opportunity whenever time permits; otherwise, they will most likely forget the correction by the time they take their next class.

Teachers will sometimes give a litany of corrections. Giving too many corrections at once can overwhelm students. This is especially relevant for children and beginners. Incorporating corrections is not easy when your students have sequence and other mechanics to think about. So allow your students time to assimilate and develop the needed muscle memory by giving one or two corrections at a time that apply to a certain step or to their placement. After you see that the correction has been understood and correctly applied, additional ones can then be given. As a student advances and has greater control over his/her body, there will be a correspondingly greater capacity for absorbing multiple corrections.

Finally, it is okay to sit down briefly. But don't plunk yourself down in a chair and only get up to demonstrate the next exercise—which is what I see many teachers do. You cannot adequately see whether a student is working correctly when you are halfway across the studio obliquely observing their posture and placement, particularly during the barre work. Let your students know that you are engaged in their class by walking around the studio, watching, giving corrections, and making individual eye contact with them. Let your students feel your energy and your desire to teach them.

Pacing

Pacing is how you utilize your studio time—how slowly or quickly you teach and complete each of the sections of your lesson plan. This is one of the most difficult teaching elements to master, and for some, it is a constant scenario of racing against the clock.

Succeeding in completing your lesson plan most of the time is very important. Many of my student teachers would ask how one can demonstrate and give explanations, plus allow students time to repeat steps and apply corrections, and still teach a complete class. It is a balancing act, no doubt! I can recall some of my old school Russian teachers who did not have any difficulty teaching a complete (and very difficult) class. This was because they rarely took the time to give any explanations about technique and give a correction. They had many set barre exercises and center floor combinations that regular attendees knew by heart, so little time was spent learning new ones. But times have changed, along with the way ballet is taught.

Successful pacing means the completion of your lesson plan within its designated time frame while allotting adequate time for a full barre and for all the sections of center floor (adagio, turns, and jumps). Let us take, for example, a 90–minute class at the intermediate level or higher: the barre work should be completed in 35–40 minutes or less, leaving at least 50 minutes for center work.

The pacing of your class should remain as consistent as possible. It should not drag and get hung up on a single learning issue and then become wildly rushed in order to fit in all of the combinations and exercises in your lesson plan. Nor should you move your class at a frenzied pace without taking the time to thoroughly teach and correct students. It's about establishing equilibrium in your time frame and keeping a watchful eye on the clock.

Your class is divided into the two sections of barre and center with a pre-determined allotment of time for each. Always be aware of how much of your lesson plan must still be completed within the remaining time for that section.

As we saw in chapter 2, adult beginners and lower-level children's classes require longer and more detailed explanations as well as the time to perform a step. Extended periods at the barre are often required. Teaching these levels requires a short and simple lesson plan.

Keeping intermediate to advanced students, who have been thoroughly taught all the necessary exercises, at the barre for an hour and then rushing through or even deleting center combinations to make up for lost time is not a model for good pacing. Of course, barre work is essential, especially in the early years of training when a good deal of the class must be devoted to learning and perfecting each of the exercises along with initially learning new center floor steps. But after a while, staying there too long can seem like drudgery to your students. Dancing is movement, and that feeling of moving though space is exhilarating. Adequate time must be given to this. Center floor is where students learn to move, and as they advance, it becomes the primary portion of the class. If you are consistently rushing or running out of time at the end of class, or if you find that more time is required to concentrate on a technical problem or to learn a new step, then you must adjust your lesson plan.

It is imperative that students understand what is being taught. But keep in mind that ballet training is a long sequential process that requires repetition and continual reinforcement from class to class. Don't let your class become bogged down with too much talk and not enough dancing. Demonstrating each exercise along with explaining the proper technique of a step and then correcting students is an essential part of good teaching. It requires a major portion of time, and it strongly impacts your pacing. Knowing how much time to spend on a subject or correction before moving on makes teaching a balancing act. Students have different learning curves, and if too much time is spent on demonstration and discussion or on a particular section of the class, you will not be able to get through your lesson plan. Giving more time to an exercise or section of the class means stealing time from another.

Ballet students learn by doing—by dancing—much more than by standing still, listening to theory and watching demonstrations, even though these are important elements. Hence the importance of concise demonstrations and explanations, thereby giving students more time to dance. New teachers often give far too much information at one time for their students to mentally process and physically apply it.

It is important to know how much to communicate. It is equally important to keep one eye on the clock while having a pacing mantra of "move along."

Using Your Voice, Demeanor, and Energy Level

The ballet studio is the teacher's absolute domain. You are in control, and therefore you establish the levels of expectation that set the overall atmosphere of the class. This atmosphere should always be alive and dynamic. When you have energy and enthusiasm in your teaching, you can rightly expect your students to dance with energy and enthusiasm.

A class of 15 to 20 students has the potential to be much more highly energized than a smaller class of 6 to 8 students (and therefore usually a lot more fun to teach). But it is you—through your demeanor and magnetism and voice—who must establish and maintain the energy and focus of the class. A greater number of students simply makes it easier.

And even though it is easier to establish and maintain a productive level of energy when there are 16 students in class as opposed to 6, you still must create an inspiring atmosphere of energy for those 6, nevertheless. Your demeanor and enthusiasm should not be based on how many students you have. Conversely, one should not infer that your class must maintain a fever pitch the entire time. That could be counterproductive. Energy level along with pacing should have ebb and flow.

The varying levels and intensity of energy are generated and controlled by your personal magnetism and communicated via your voice with its volume, inflection, and cadence, along with the carriage and expression of your body, the manner in which you speak to students, and the way you demonstrate. However you present yourself in class—highly energetic, inspiring, encouraging, demanding, or lackadaisical, indifferent, enervating—students will respond accordingly. Take the time to look at and read the body language of your students. It will often and accurately reflect your own demeanor and energy level.

Almost everyone has had a teacher who lectured in a monotone. Listening to that hypnotic drone quickly saps all interest and enthusiasm for the subject matter, and eventually it can bring on sleep.

Vocal dynamics, just like movement dynamics, are controlled and altered according to the degree of force—energy—infused in it. Therefore, your voice and the overall energy level of your class are interrelated.

The voice is a teacher's most powerful asset for delivery of his/her class. And it too should have an ebb and flow using modulation—varying your pitch, intensity, and tone. Through inflective nuance and modulation, the dynamic ability of your voice has enormous range and power to communicate the technical and artistic dynamics of ballet. It can positively impact every aspect of your teaching.

Most important, your voice must sound natural and appropriate for each type and level of class you teach. Along with your demeanor, it should have the proper degree of maturity for the age group. Never talk down to students. Modify your volume according to how many students you have in the studio so you can be heard by everyone, and do not speak to a class of 8 students with the same volume and energy you would use in a larger studio with a class of 28. Be aware of extremes with inflection so that your voice does not go up and down the vocal scale like a kazoo. Most assuredly, that is the opposite extreme from monotone on the irritability scale!

It is good pedagogical practice, especially for a new teacher, to occasionally record your voice during a class so you can analyze your modulations and dynamics. It is a great personal teaching tool, as is videotaping your teaching, humbling though it may be.

Using Music Effectively

The ability to move musically with grace, aplomb, and dynamism as well as with great speed and accuracy—these are the goals of the advanced dancer. To be successful at this, you need an appropriately chosen meter and tempo in order for your students to have time to perfect all aspects of their technique. This includes getting into and out of precise and clean positions, using feet correctly, using the *demi-plié*, coordinating connecting steps with primary steps in movement phrases, developing good elevation, and incorporating the use of *épaulement* and *port de bras*.

One of the most important pedagogical skills for teaching ballet is knowing how to properly and effectively use music. The music you choose for each exercise and combination will strongly impact the successful outcome of your class. Potentially fine combinations are unsuccessful in accomplishing their training objectives because the tempo is either too fast or too slow or the meter and type of music are wrong. By choosing the correct tempo, meter, and rhythm, you enable your students to perform combinations with technical precision, the correct dynamics, and musicality. For instance, in terms of tempo, an adagio sequence must be slow enough for students to build strength and control and to feel the classical lines of the positions. But if done too slowly, it may look heavy and static, caused by gripping tension in the muscles. Or with meter, giving a broad swinging movement as in a *grand battement en cloche* to a 4/4 march may not work as effectively as a 6/8 meter or a lively 3/4 waltz.

Two components create dynamic quality in dance movement: force and time. Force is the degree of effort or energy that is being used by giving accent to a movement. Time is the speed, how fast or slow the step is done. For example, if the dynamics of an *allegro* combination have the qualities of high elevation with suspension and *ballon* (bouncing), then the use of a triple meter such as a broad 6/8 or certain 3/4's may work best. But if the rebounding quality of a jump is percussive, quick, and sharp, a duple meter of 2/4 would be more conducive. Once the appropriate meter is chosen, the tempo is then determined and set. (Chapter 4 addresses meter and musical structure in more detail.)

Setting a suitable tempo (speed) is one of the biggest difficulties I see when I observe classes. The problem is compounded when CDs are used without a variable speed player. Technical precision cannot be accomplished if the tempo is incorrect. In the case of *allegro*, it is usually too fast.

It is imperative for teachers to understand meter and to be familiar with common types of music used in the studio, such as waltz, mazurka, march, polonaise, tango, polka, gallop, and various types of adagio. I often see young teachers confuse meter and tempo, thinking they are interchangeable. When a combination doesn't work correctly with the music, s/he will ask the pianist to slow down or speed up the tempo when, in fact, the problem has to do with incorrect meter. If you want a *petit allegro* combination to have *ballon*, a 2/4 or 4/4 meter might not be appropriate, regardless of tempo. Choosing a 6/8 or some other triple meter would be a better choice. Even though a 6/8 meter can often sound like a 2/4 because the first and fourth beats of the measure are accented (**1** 2 3 **4** 5 6), a musical dancer and teacher can feel the difference between dancing a combination that is played with a 2/4 meter and dancing to a 6/8 meter at the same tempo. This is because the structure and dynamics of the triple meter give a feeling of bounce and thus suspension to the performance of the movement.

Then there is rhythm—the type of music that would work best for a particular exercise or combination. Does a strong 3/4 mazurka fit the rhythmical dynamics of your turning combination better than a 3/4 lyrical waltz? Perhaps a polka rather than a gallop better supports the diagonal *piqué* and *chaîné* turns. Using a grand waltz for diagonal *grand jetés* across the floor requires strong elevation that less advanced students do not have. So choosing a quick waltz, or even a 2/4 rag, will better support the students' elevation abilities and will require only slight adjustments in tempo.

Becoming educated and experienced with meter and rhythm in the classroom takes time, practice, and a sensitive ear. Having a good, **experienced** pianist always makes it a lot easier. But when you teach only with recorded music, you are limited to whatever selections the CD offers. Nevertheless, there are some very good ballet CDs with a wide range of selections. Using more than one CD for a class is advisable because it will give you a broader and richer selection of music. The best way to learn and gather experience is to spend a lot of time listening and experimenting with your combinations to the music tracks of differing meters and rhythms and then analyzing how they vary and change the dynamics of the movement and which track best accomplishes the objective of the combination.

Lastly, be aware of the music volume level when working with recorded music. Don't be in competition with your music by having it too loud, making it difficult or impossible for your students to hear you. Conversely, volume that is too soft will cause or contribute to a low energy level. So find a comfortable balance between your voice and the music.

Teaching through Touch

As the piano is the instrument that a pianist must master, the human body is the instrument that the dancer must master. The well-trained dancer is required to strengthen and thoroughly train his/her arms, legs, feet, torso, and head so that they can be moved with isolation and in harmonious coordination to whatever demands the choreographic composition presents. Students therefore rely on their teacher to identify misalignment in their anatomical placement and posture and to correct technical errors in their dancing.

Children and older beginning students who have not yet developed a good sense of body awareness sometimes find it difficult to apply corrections that are given verbally, other than the most simplistic concrete ones, and even then for some it is a challenge. And as I stated previously, it is important for a student to kinesthetically feel what is correct opposed to incorrect, and that often requires you to physically adjust your student's body. Touch can be the most efficient and straightforward way to make most anatomical placement and postural corrections. As a student gains knowledge and control over his/her body and learns more anatomical terminology, certain verbal corrections usually can be given. But many corrections in dance are subtle, and they require nuance in adjustments that can best be given by your touch.

Young children and adolescents will react variously to touch depending on how they have been raised and the particular state and development of their psyche. Boys and girls who are in an intensive preprofessional training program with aspirations for a dance career will rarely have an issue with correction by touch. In fact, these types of personalized corrections are regarded in a positive way as being individually noticed and given special attention.

Parents, children, and adolescent girls are generally more at ease with and therefore more accepting of physical contact from a female teacher than from a male teacher. This is especially true with many pubescent girls because they are particularly sensitive to their changing bodies—hormones are affecting them physically and psychologically. This is when we begin to see all of the camouflage clothing being worn to class, covering up developing breasts and hips and often weight gain. Every girl has a different biological clock that will ultimately determine how long it will take her to adjust to her physiological changes. Teachers need to be sensitive to their students' physiological development.

Professional dancers and teachers do not give the teaching through touch adjustments a second thought, because we regard our bodies as the instruments of our art form, and this is how we were trained every day for years. Also, as dancers, we become used to being touched and touching each other through choreography and *pas de deux* work (partnering).

Touching in ballet training or in a rehearsal should never be sexually construed any more than a doctor's touch is during a physical exam or with the manipulations of a physical therapist. However, ballet teachers are not perceived in the same way as doctors and therapists. And we must always be aware that we live in an overly litigious society and that the average parent is oblivious to what is considered necessary and normal physical contact during a ballet class. Anyone not familiar with formal ballet training may see and interpret this type of contact with a student as sexually provocative because it often includes touching the rib cage, top of the sternum (breast bone) and collar bones, abdomen, sacrum, thighs, and buttocks. Seemingly less provocative areas are the lower legs and feet, arms and hands, shoulders, and head.

As absurd as it may sound, a parent can misinterpret a common physical correction as an inappropriate or sexually motivated touch. Regrettably, many teachers have chosen not to touch at all as a teaching tool or only to touch students on the arms, feet, shoulders, and head. Other teachers are very careful to touch and adjust students using only one finger, never the whole hand. Numerous dance programs in public and magnet schools have been forced to initiate an absolute policy of no physical contact between teachers and students in the dance studio. As a result, the quality and integrity of teaching is often greatly diminished. This is a tragic development in the long and illustrious development of ballet training.

It is important to be aware of the mind-set of our culture and to make decisions accordingly. Many private studios and schools are now requiring their parents and adult students to sign an injury release waiver and a statement that acknowledges the necessity to make physical corrections and adjustments through touch in order to correct faulty placement and technique and to minimize the risk of injury associated with dance training. It is always advisable to get legal advice concerning the proper wording of waivers from a qualified attorney and to have adequate liability insurance coverage.

A receptive and sensitive teacher will know if a student feels uncomfortable with being touched and will be responsive to how, or if, touch should be used.

Touch is an immensely powerful way to communicate in your teaching. Never ever touch a student in an angry, negative, or scolding way. Always correct and adjust using a positive, compassionate, and nurturing approach.

Teaching with Imagery

Teachers can employ various approaches to teaching and correcting their students—through demonstration, touch, musical phrasing and rhythm, and imagery.

We may use just one or a combination of these skills. Not all students, though, will have a positive response in a like manner when you communicate the same directive. One student will be more receptive to a tactile kinesthetic correction and to a specific concrete anatomical reference point, while another will react more effectively to an abstract visualization.

The musculoskeletal structure of one dancer is different from that of the next, and every dancer moves in his or her own unique way expressing individual feelings and understanding of technique within the same classical ballet vocabulary. This diversity can make it challenging for a teacher to connect with each student using the most effective and succinct method. But over time, the teacher will know how each student responds best to a particular teaching approach. If 8 out of 10 dancers connect to a given imagery directive, then for those remaining 2, a different image, explanation, or touch will have to be found that they can relate to and understand.

Dance imagery is visually descriptive language that a teacher employs to create a specific kinesthetic feeling and picture in the mind of the dancer that will lead to the right technical or artistic response. It can be very simple and literal where a child can picture and apply it, or the image and concept can be rather abstract.

Using imagery effectively is a sophisticated teaching skill that calls upon the teacher's intuitive sense and imagination. Imagery guides the student to visualize or imagine and sometimes **feel** an image within the body or even outside the body that will facilitate the correct use of dynamic movement quality and an accuracy and purity of technique and line. For instance, visualizing the feeling of a spiral during a pirouette is a very effective image—each turn spirals **up** to the next higher level. The dancer's actual kinesthetic action in order to do this is the strong force of pushing **down** through the supporting leg against the resistance of the floor in the opposite direction of the upward, spiraling movement image. Anatomically and technically, this helps the dancer resist any sinking into the supporting hip and maximizes the lift in his/her center of gravity, thus supporting the successful execution of multiple pirouettes.

This downward force is the same feeling one has while holding a stationary balance as well. The balance relates a look of stillness, a pose of stability, while that stable feeling for the dancer, internally, is quite dynamic—always pushing down, moving against the weight and force of gravity within that illusion of stillness.

The interpretation of all of these words—pushing, stillness, spiraling, the feeling of dynamic force projected in various energy patterns—contributes to developing a visualization and feeling that can be different for each dancer and also quite effective.

Imagining patterns of energy internally and projecting it externally is effective and powerful imagery. Combining it with the dancer's visual focus—the powerful use of the eyes—can further project a movement outward beyond the parameters of the physical body. It is how a dancer projects movement and gesture past the footlights, well into the audience. It also gives life and dynamism to classical line and movement.

Imagery can be quite simplistic. Vera Volkova, one of the foremost teachers of the Vaganova system, in order to keep her young girls from sinking into their chests, would tell them to imagine that they were wearing a magnificent necklace of diamonds, emeralds, and rubies that covered their neck and upper chest and that they must keep the carriage of their chest lifted proudly to show off the jewels. That automatically establishes reference points for them at the sternum/solar plexus and the point between the shoulder blades that controls the upper torso.

We learn in physics class that "every action has an equal and opposite reaction." All physical movement requires two forces working in opposition to each other. Even classical poses and positions maintain a dynamic look by the oppositional lengthening force of their lines. For example, an *arabesque* has two distinct patterns of oppositional forces of energy: the up/down force through the supporting leg and torso that keeps the *arabesque* lifted to its highest point and gives stability, and the horizontal force of the front arm, solar plexus, and visual focus, against the opposing direction of the elevated working leg and back arm.

Another example of opposing forces that give stability and maintain balance is the *grand battement*. Visualize a curving pattern of energy as the working foot brushes out of fifth position and the leg flies into the air, while a simultaneous pattern of energy moves down through the supporting leg pushing against the floor, thus resisting with equal force the movement of the working leg and giving equal stability to both legs and torso. As the working leg descends using eccentric contraction, the supporting leg continues to lengthen, pushing downward into the floor, causing the center of gravity to remain lifted with the desired look of the upper carriage.

If you choose to use imagery as a regular approach to teaching, make sure that what you say is clear to your students. Some teachers come out with phrases that are vague or esoteric, leaving their students confused. Visualization and metaphor can be quite simple: "let's imagine today that you are performing this center floor combination before a large audience"; "feel that you are doing slow controlled *relevés* on eggshells"; "feel the fluidity of the *port de bras* while imagining that the arms are made of chiffon"; "visualize the compression of a coiled spring between the legs on the landing from a jump and the release of the spring's tension on the next jump."

Avoid using negative or debasing imagery to make a correction. I have had teachers who used sardonic imagery, but it only works with teachers who know how to infuse it with a humorous tone and employ it in classes generally populated by advanced and/or mature students and without directing it personally at a dancer.

Imagery is a complex and comprehensive teaching skill. Teachers spend their entire careers developing, renewing, and refining it. Watching our colleagues teach can be valuable and rejuvenating because we hear fresh ways to teach and make corrections through different images and metaphors. One of the most thorough books written on this subject for both ballet and modern dance is *Dance Imagery for Technique and Performance* by Eric Franklin.

7

Dancer Health and Injuries

Ballet has long been called a plastic art because the dancer-artist communicates the creative ideas of the choreographer as a moving sculpture. There is nothing natural about classical ballet and the various positions and movements that are required of the dancer. For that reason, training at the pre-professional level with the intention of becoming a professional dancer is not appropriate for everyone, and when it is pursued wholeheartedly, it will lead to injury for some.

Ballet is highly cultured and sophisticated in its technical demands. For accuracy of execution, each step in its vocabulary requires that the legs and feet be turned out and that there be excellent flexibility in the hips and torso. Therefore, ballet requires a body that is strong and supple and one that has the ability to shape itself and move in accordance with classic line and technique. This is why it is so important for aspiring dancers to begin training at a young age when there is a good degree of natural flexibility and when ligaments can be slightly stretched while muscles are strengthened and stretched.

Students develop increased flexibility in the legs, feet, and torso by gradually coaxing their bodies to flex, extend, and rotate. However, not all students are successful in accomplishing this goal because, even at a young age, their bodies are not naturally and easily responsive to the demands of ballet. Some students find that they need to use excessive, perpetually held force to hold and control positions, and this can result in various types of injuries.

Aches and Pains

Aches and pains are expected in any kind of intense physical training and throughout a ballet dancer's performing career. However, there are good aches and pains resulting from developing strength and flexibility through proper training, and there are bad aches and pains that predict an injury. Bad pain might be sharp, shooting, radiating, or burning from inflammation. It can be localized or radiate to other parts of the body.

The source of good pain is from muscles and fascia as a result of stretching or heavily working a muscle group. It is generalized and does not feel sharp or inflamed. Intense or prolonged exercise causes the muscle tissue fibers to break down. After a short period of recovery, the repaired muscle fibers rebound, making it a stronger muscle than before. In the meantime, the muscles may feel sore; lactic acid buildup resulting from exercising will complicate the recovery and discomfort level. Stretching and frequent massaging are beneficial, as they help to break up the lactic acid within the muscle. Also, keeping the body well hydrated will speed up recovery.

It is important for dancers to get thoroughly warmed up in order to reduce the chances of injury. It takes approximately 20–30 minutes to completely warm up muscles, so coming to class early in order to begin warming up should be encouraged. Once the muscles are warmed (in the latter part of barre work), it is then safe to do full stretches.

We read in chapter 3 that fascia is connective tissue that covers the muscles, tendons, and ligaments. It has elastic qualities, and part of its structure is made up of a gelatinous substance known as collagen. These firm gelatinous collagen fibers soften and flow when the fascia becomes warm. This enables a greater and more comfortable range of movement. Notice how during cold winter months the body generally feels stiff and tight before class but much less so during the warmer months. This is due to the warmth or coldness (stiffness) of the fascia. Risk of injury is greater when the muscles and fascia are cold. This is why it is so important for dancers to warm up before a rehearsal if they have not had a previous class and to take the time to stretch at the end of their dancing. Overly zealous stretching, as well as stretching when the muscles and fascia are cold, can cause slight tears in the fascia. These microscopic tears usually heal quickly, though the feeling of soreness can be acute. Intense over-stretching should be avoided, as it can severely tear soft tissue and cause serious injury, which will require a longer recovery time.

Injuries can be simply the result of accidents such as slips and falls. Bad luck! Sometimes they are caused by poor dance floors and surfaces. Deficient or misunderstood training and poor execution of technique largely contribute to most injuries, and they are, more often than not, due to bad musculoskeletal alignment, which puts strain on the joints and causes improper development of the muscles. The human body is capable of a lot of demands and punishment during training, but it is not made of steel. Eventually something tears, snaps, breaks, or burns. And when it does, it is usually the result of months or even years of improper alignment and poor technique.

I recall incessantly correcting a student to keep her supporting knee and thigh in alignment with her foot when landing on one leg from a jump. This was a deeply ingrained bad habit. Either her previous teachers had never corrected her or she had not been diligent enough in applying the correction. When she phoned to tell me that she had torn her anterior cruciate ligament (ACL) at summer school, she was surprised that I immediately knew which knee she had injured. An injury was inevitable. And so by not correcting this alignment issue she was indeed forced to learn the hard way through a very serious injury—one that could end a performing career.

A new student in my university program told me that for more than a year she had not been able to take class without having pain in her left ankle and Achilles tendon. When I adjusted her alignment over her foot, the pain immediately subsided. She had been gripping her foot and ankle in order to hold her balance, triggered by improperly placed alignment, which caused undue stress on her muscles, tendons, and ligaments. She had been standing this way, class after class, for more than a year. Gone uncorrected, this would undoubtedly have turned into a chronic injury such as tendonitis or a stress fracture in the foot or ankle.

Unfortunately, many students think that injuries are unavoidable, particularly with pointe work. This is not so! While dance injuries are a fact of life for many dancers, there are many others who have had long injury-free careers.

Harmful habits also contribute to the frequency of injuries. These include smoking, poor diet, inadequate sleep, dehydration, and drug and alcohol abuse. Other factors of injury include muscular imbalance, fatigue, excessive body weight, growth spurts where the bones grow faster than the muscles, and hormonal changes triggered by stress or puberty, which cause muscles to tighten. Emotional and psychological problems can exacerbate or be the cause of poor physical health and eating disorders.

Five areas of the body are most prone to dance injuries: ankle and foot, knee, hamstring, hip, and back. Fractures, strains, and sprains are acute traumatic injuries that are particularly common. Fractures are breaks in the bone tissue and can be as severe as a complete break or just a hair-line stress fracture. Most fractures in dancers occur in the feet (particularly metatarsals and sesamoid bones), ankles, and shins. A strain is a tear in the muscle—a soft tissue injury. Many strains happen in the hamstrings and other muscles of the thigh and hip area. A sprain is a tear in a ligament, the connective tissue that binds bones together at a joint. They happen most frequently in the dancer's ankle, foot, and knee. Sprains are often accompanied by muscle tissue strains. Common sprains of the knee are tears in the anterior cruciate ligament (ACL), medial collateral ligament (MCL), and cartilage (meniscus).

The most common chronic injury in dancers is tendonitis—inflammation of a tendon, which connects muscle to bone. There are two types of tendonitis that are most prevalent to dancers: **Dancer's tendonitis** is inflammation of the flexor tendon of the big toe (FLH tendon). It flexes the big toe and runs the length of the foot and behind the ankle. It can cause pain in the arch, big toe, or ankle. **Achilles tendonitis** is inflammation of the tendon that connects the calf muscle to the heel bone. Tearing of the Achilles tendon is an injury that plagues professional dancers because of its seriousness. Many careers have ended as a result of complete rupture of the Achilles.

To avoid tendonitis, teachers must carefully watch and ensure that their students bring their heels down when doing pointe work and when landing from jumps, and correct overcrossed and forced fifth positions, especially when taking off and landing from jumps and *relevés*.

One other common injury that can become chronic is **shin splints**. This is very uncomfortable muscle pain in the lower leg that is attributed to one or all of the following: dancing on very hard floors, improper use of *plié* in jumps, including gripping the feet and ankles and failing to get one's heels down, skeletal misalignment on takeoff and landing from jumps, and forcing too much rotation of the feet at the ankles. Shin splints can also lead to small stress fractures in the bone. Some of my students have had stress fractures that were misdiagnosed and treated as shin splints because they were very hard to identify on X-rays. Applying a cold pack or alternating heat and cold will most likely feel soothing but will not cure the condition. The only way to alleviate shin splints is simply to rest, take time off, or refrain from jumps for a period of time.

Treating Injuries

Many injuries are less severe when a dancer receives early correct diagnosis followed by proper treatment from an orthopedic doctor familiar with the rigors of dance training and when an effective rehabilitation regimen is followed that often includes altering and correcting anatomical alignment. Rehabilitation is important to prevent repeat injuries by addressing and treating any lingering problems, and this should be done by a physiotherapist who has a thorough understanding of dance injuries and ballet technique. It is also advisable that the physiotherapist, dancer, and teacher are in regular communication with each other.

The ballet teacher is usually the first person students come to when aches and pains develop, an injury of some sort is suspected, or the demonstrable accident/injury happens during class. Your students look to you to guide them. It is all right to address the many minor complaints that we regularly encounter in the ballet studio. The universally recommended standard course of treatment for most of these is Rest, Ice, Compression, and Elevation (RICE). Rest means to temporarily stop dancing. A cold pack or bag of ice wrapped in a cloth or towel should be applied directly to the injured area; the cloth prevents the skin from freezing. Use compression by wrapping a pressure bandage (not too tightly) over the cold pack. Elevate the injured part above the level of the heart.

When in doubt whether to use ice or heat, always choose ice. Icing is the regularly accepted therapeutic practice at the outset of an injury or discomfort because it helps to eliminate any swelling caused by excessive accumulation of blood at the site of the injury. Inflammation, or swelling, is a natural bodily process for healing, but too much swelling is not good because it causes excessive scar tissue to develop. For common classroom injuries such as a sprained ankle, immediately apply ice or a cold pack and elevate the leg. Elevation and compression also aid in reducing swelling, hence RICE. Once the initial swelling has subsided, usually over a day or more, heat and cold can be applied. Applying alternating heat and cold causes an ebb and flow exchange of fluids and brings healing fresh blood to the area. Massage is another important treatment therapy because it helps to move the edema, or swelling, out of the injured area.

Always recommend that your student see a doctor when there is an acute injury such as an ankle sprain, suspected fracture, or a chronic or potentially chronic condition like tendonitis. Otherwise, for the minor aches and pains, the standard treatments are pretty safe.

Be aware that an accurate diagnosis of the problem is crucial to successfully treating it. Always recommend that your students seek professional medical advice if you, the student, or a parent has the slightest hunch that the pain or injury is serious or potentially serious or if it is a chronic complaint. **Never** assume the role of a doctor or physical therapist and prescribe treatment as if you were dispensing medical advice! Otherwise, you could find yourself on the slippery slope headed toward a lawsuit.

Many dance schools have one or two orthopedic doctors and a physical therapist who have experience treating dance injuries and to whom they can refer their students. Also, all dance schools should have a first aid kit to treat the occasional cut, bleeding blister, or acute traumatic injuries. It should contain sterile gloves, hydrogen peroxide, bandages, gauze, medical tape, topical antibacterial cream, an ACE bandage, and a few instant cold packs.

A brief word about studio hygiene is also in order. As dancers work hard in class, they sweat, some quite profusely. Perspiration can contain a host of bacteria and viruses that can easily be spread to others by touching the ballet barre and each other. This cannot be helped, but keeping a clean studio, which includes frequently washing the floor and wiping down the barres with bleach or a cleaner/disinfectant product, will go a long way in stopping the spread of germs. Teachers should wash their hands immediately after every class—especially if they correct their students by touching them—and/or have a bottle of antimicrobial gel such as Purell in the studio. Teachers should also encourage their students to wash their hands right after class.

Nutrition and Eating Disorders

Parents of serious ballet students often will ask their teachers for advice regarding proper nutrition, and so teachers should take the time to educate themselves in this integral segment of a student's training. The importance of good nutrition is an often neglected part of ballet training. Many dancers, students and professionals, do not realize how necessary proper nutrition is to their physical development—the right balance of proteins, fats, and carbohydrates along with enough caloric intake and sufficient hydration. Inadequate nutrition can contribute to injuries, as bones and muscles must have the proper nutrients to initially grow and develop and then to maintain and repair themselves.

There are general standards for the percentages of nutrients we should consume each day, which are approximately 15 percent protein, 25 percent fat, and 60 percent carbohydrates. I dare say that few of us keep a running tally of what we eat, plus the breakdown of these three components, and how many calories we consume—nor are many of us likely to start now. Using common sense and establishing a healthy diet of multiple daily meals consisting of fresh fruits and vegetables, whole grains, unsaturated fats such as olive oil, lean meats, skinless chicken, fish, and soy or wheat gluten (tofu and seitan) for the vegetarians will give the dancer the needed building blocks for a strong and healthy body. We should drink plenty of fluids, water always being the best source; a minimum of eight 8–ounce glasses of water is the universal daily recommendation. Fast foods should never be a regular source of nutrition, nor much of the prepared foods found in grocery stores. Most of these foods are extremely high in sodium, sugar and unhealthy fats.

Ballet dancers, especially girls, are expected to have a very lean body, not unlike that of an Olympic distance runner or gymnast. But unlike distance running, ballet is not all that aerobic—dancers mostly move through bursts of energy much like a sprinter with intermittent rests, and so they do not burn the number of calories that one might think. Therefore, watching caloric intake is always on their minds. The number of calories burned in ratio to one's daily caloric intake determines whether weight is gained, lost, or unchanged.

Too few schools give nutritional advice to young dancers, including the ubiquitous summer ballet intensives throughout the country. Each year I see girls in summer intensives who go to their early morning class without having breakfast and then go through most of the day taking multiple classes while eating little or nothing at all until they have their evening meal. They erroneously think that this will keep them from gaining weight. What they do not realize is that when the body is denied nutrition, it sends the message that it is being starved, and it then begins to take needed nutrition from its own muscles, bones, and stored fat—the body essentially **eats** itself. This is counterproductive to building muscle tissue and strength. Also, during a biological **starvation alert,** the body lowers its rate of metabolism so that when the dancer does eventually eat, fewer calories are burned and the remaining ones are stored as fat reserves. If that one meal at the end of the day contains a large amount of calories, there is more likelihood of experiencing actual weight gain instead of loss.

Then there are the girls who take an intelligent approach to eating and maintaining a proper weight. They have a light breakfast before morning class, preferably one high in protein, and they pack food in their dance bag so that they can **graze** between classes and rehearsals throughout the day. This would include things like fresh fruit, cut-up raw vegetables, low-fat yogurt and string cheese (lots of protein and calcium!), low-fat granola, a hardboiled egg, nuts-seeds-dried fruit or trail mix, etc. Eating small amounts throughout the day gives the body continual nourishment and keeps its metabolic rate from plunging. Maintaining a good metabolism means that maximum calories are being burned, and when those larger meals are eaten, there is less chance of weight gain.

Another subject that impacts a dancer's health is that of eating disorders: anorexia and bulimia. Both conditions can be caused by psychological, sociological, or neurobiological components or a combination of any of these. They are prevalent conditions in the dance world, and the onset can begin in adolescence as young as 13, mostly with girls, although boys are not immune. Approximately 10 percent of all people with eating disorders are male.

Bulimia is an illness that is characterized by excessive overeating or binge eating followed by purging. Purging is primarily self-induced vomiting, but it can also include the use of laxatives, diuretics, and enemas to rapidly remove food before it is digested. Dancers suffering from bulimia can be hard to detect because they usually don't show any immediate signs of ill health or drastic weight loss.

Anorexia is an illness characterized by low body weight, an obsessive fear of gaining weight, and a distorted body image. Dancers suffering from anorexia will try to control their weight through starvation, purging, diet pills, and extreme exercise. Bulimia is often part of the anorexic disorder. It is much easier to detect anorexia because of the associated weight loss. Anorexia is a very serious illness, as people can and do die from it.

A dancer who is suffering from an eating disorder needs the immediate help of a medical professional. Anorexic and bulimic dancers will rarely admit that they have an eating disorder, and they will do or say anything to convince their teachers and parents that they are not purging or starving themselves. A teacher who suspects that his/her student has this illness should bring it to the attention of the parents or, in the case of students 18 years or older, speak with the student and encourage her to get medical help. It is especially difficult for those who teach in a university, because privacy laws prohibit teachers or institutions from communicating to parents anything concerning a student's academic performance or welfare without the written permission of that student.

In the private studio sector, developing good relationships with parents and having regular teacher/parent conferences can contribute to a better training environment. Establishing a good rapport with parents makes communications easier when difficult situations such as eating disorders, behavioral problems, or learning disorders arise and disrupt their child's dance training.

8

Establishing
Your Own School

Laying the Groundwork

Many private studio teachers prefer to work for an employer rather than cope with all of the responsibilities of owning their own business. But for entrepreneurial minded teachers, this chapter is devoted to opening and operating a dance school enterprise.

Your first decision is to determine what type of school you want. Will it be a studio with a commercial focus that enthusiastically participates in regional and national dance competitions, or one that is geared to a more formal preprofessional curriculum? Will you present recitals, and if so, how will that fit into the training curriculum? What other dance forms will you offer besides ballet—jazz, hip-hop, tap, modern dance? Will you also offer classes in Yoga and Pilates? Do you have experienced, qualified teachers for what you offer? In most schools the highest revenue producers, after ballet, are jazz and hip-hop. This is important when planning your class schedule and revenue projections.

Revenue from a studio comes from tuition and other ancillary sources. Recital participation fees, costume fees, and ticket sales along with the sale of performance videos or DVDs can substantially increase overall revenue. Many schools have boutiques that sell dance shoes and various types of clothing, including apparel with the studio name/logo on them—a great, inexpensive way to advertise your school.

Advertising is very important, especially with the opening of your school and before the beginning of each school year and summer session. This would be in the form of direct mailings of brochures and schedules and advertisements in local newspapers and periodicals. Once you are recognized, your best advertising is always word-of-mouth by establishing a reputation for quality and excellence in your dance training. Additionally, a user-friendly website is essential, and it should have a map and directions to your location, class schedule, calendar, tuition fees, studio policies, performance information, faculty biographies, and contact information.

Parents can be very demanding, sometimes with special circumstances pertaining to their children. Such parents and the occasional errant behavior of students are frequently exasperating. Therefore, I strongly advise writing the most comprehensive handbook of studio policies possible that students and parents must agree to by a parental or adult-student signature.

Some recommended policies are:

- Tuition fees, discounts, payment plans, and refund/credit policies
- Makeup classes
- Class placement
- Proper studio etiquette and behavior
- Proper dance attire and hairstyle
- Attendance
- Class observations and "parents' week."
- Class cancellation and rescheduling
- Lost and found items
- Signature certifying that student is healthy and able to participate in dance class
- Liability release for personal injury, illness, and property loss or damage

Location and Demographics

Two important considerations in opening a dance school are location and demographics. When searching for a studio location, square footage is a priority along with the ability to expand. A small studio will limit your enrollment (and income) and will inhibit teaching the large traveling movements.

In an urban area, is there public transportation nearby? And in a suburban or rural area, is the building easily accessible from the street or highway and will there be sufficient parking or auto waiting areas?

What is your market? How many children live in your area, and how many other dance schools are competing for the same students? Check the number of lower and middle schools plus the enrollment size of public, private, and parochial high schools. Is there a baby boom in the area? Does your area have potential for growth? What are the economic strata?

Locating in a commercial building in a retail area or shopping center, especially on street level, will most likely cost the most per square foot; therefore, it is not always the best choice for a start-up. We need lots of square footage for dance. Choosing a space above street level, a loft area, or a location that is off the main thoroughfare will always be cheaper per square foot.

Working with a commercial real-estate agent can save you time and energy. S/he will be able to supply some of the demographic statistics and advise you in negotiating with the landlord. Realtor commissions are usually paid by the property owner, not by the tenant.

Perhaps the easiest way is to buy a school that has been established for some time and that has a good reputation, healthy enrollment numbers, and a good working facility. However, this might require considerable capital, depending on how many students are enrolled and how profitable the school has been.

Another way to start is by renting a large room from a church, community center, or social organization such as the Lions Club, Elks, or American Legion. Try to find a space that has a buoyant floor and a good surface. There is usually a reasonable flat rental fee for this type of space rather than a calculated dollar amount for each square foot. So if you can't or don't want to make a large upfront investment, this is a good, conservative way to begin your school and thereby establish a clientele that will be your revenue base when you decide to have your own permanent location.

Creating a Business Plan

Whatever your approach, starting your own school will require an investment of capital along with careful planning. If you expect to borrow money, your bank will most likely require you to submit a complete business plan. Even if you don't need a loan, you should generate for yourself a simple business plan that reflects your start-up costs and regular monthly expenses as well as your projected revenue.

The biggest capital expenditure when moving into a commercial unfinished space is the build-out: drywall partitions for the studio, reception area, office, dressing rooms, and bathroom. A sprung dance floor may be needed (if the space does not already have a buoyant wooden floor), plus a vinyl dance floor surface, mirrors, permanent wall barres and portable barres, and signage. (Sometimes it's possible to negotiate a shared expense build-out with your landlord.)

Start-up costs are mostly capital expenditures that can be depreciated and written off on your taxes over a period of years:

- Build-out (partitions, lighting, electrical wiring, etc.)
- Dance floor
- Vinyl floor surface
- Barres
- Mirrors
- Computer
- Phone system
- Audio/DVD equipment
- Furniture (office, studio chairs, dressing room and reception area benches and chairs)
- Piano

A monthly payment either to yourself (as a reimbursement) or to the bank (loan repayment) will be reflected in your monthly expenses.

- Monthly/quarterly expenses:
- Rent
- Utilities
- Phone (w/DSL)
- Custodial services
- Insurance (including liability and workers' compensation)

- Advertising
- Printing (brochure and schedules)
- Office supplies
- Teaching supplies (including music CDs and DVDs)
- Loan payment
- Payroll
- Tax preparation (accountant)
- Taxes
- Unemployment insurance and business license fees
- Legal

Once you have determined your total estimated monthly expenses, you can then decide how many students you need enrolled and how much tuition or other revenue you must bring in each month.

If you are not a one-person operation and have other faculty teaching for you, it is important to consider whether you will pay them as employees or as independent contractors. If you pay them as employees, you will be responsible for the employer's contribution to social security and state unemployment compensation insurance and for quarterly IRS and SS contributions and reporting. For independent contractors, there are no IRS and SS withholdings or unemployment insurance payments.

Full coverage insurance is a must: fire, theft, liability, and workers' compensation if there are employees. Accidents and injuries happen in dance classes, so liability insurance for any possible negligence by you or your teachers is necessary, even if they are independent contractors.

The larger your school becomes, the more important it is to have an administrative assistant or staff to handle all of the daily, weekly, and monthly responsibilities, especially if you are devoting much of your time to teaching and building enrollments. Generating new class schedules and calendars, marketing, booking a recital venue, creating rehearsal schedules, responding to inquiries and sending out studio information, returning student or parent daily phone calls, checking students in, overseeing proper cleaning and maintenance of the facility (especially the dance floor, barres, and mirrors), payroll, financial bookkeeping including accounts payable and receivable—collecting tuition from delinquent or deadbeat parents/students—trial balances and bank statements, and filing various state and federal quarterly reports are just some of the responsibilities of operating a dance school.

Last, it is advisable to incorporate for tax and accounting purposes and liability protection. There are a few corporate structures to choose from: a regular corporation, a subchapter S corporation, a limited liability corporation (LLC), or a partnership. Each type has its advantages and disadvantages regarding your corporate and personal taxes and income. Therefore, it is prudent to speak with your tax advisor or accountant before you set up a corporation. Incorporating is not difficult, and you do not necessarily need an attorney. Every state has a website with directions on how to file corporation papers.

9

A Final Word

After teaching for many years, I looked back on my training, along with the years it took to become a professional dancer, and the success I had in accomplishing my goals and having the career I had planned. It struck me that there are intrinsic characteristics or qualities in our training both in technique and performance that go far beyond merely training the body and mind to dance. Training in ballet prepares dancers for performing careers, albeit relatively short ones. But it does more than that; it also prepares them for life. It offers them what entrepreneurs possess and what corporate, educational, research, and nonprofit enterprises seek in future associates and executives.

Ballet dancers who have been comprehensively well trained are a very special group of people. No other performing artist goes through such rigorous and ongoing training or has to refine such a complicated instrument as the human body in order to express his/her art. Dancers go to class every day, week after week, month after month, and year after year, striving to master technique and to maintain elusive technical and artistic perfection. This requires a high degree of ambition and drive, the extent of which will determine the level of professional success.

What happens in this process, however, is more than just learning how to execute 32 *fouettés* or a double *tour* or to show the pure classical line in one's *arabesque*. It establishes a self-disciplined work ethic and a structure of values that make up the foundation for success, not just in ballet but in anything we choose to do. Through our training in dance technique along with ancillary studies in choreography, dance history, music fundamentals, repertoire, and performance, we learn how to think critically and analytically, to synthesize and apply knowledge and skill, and to be goal oriented and perfection driven.

Dancers understand time management. We come to class, to rehearsal, and to the theater on time and prepared. We know how to behave in our work environment because we adhere to a long history of tradition and etiquette. Dance is a collaborative art form, and so we are constantly engaged in and learning how to utilize interpersonal one-on-one skills as well as group communications that are directed at accomplishing our overall production goals.

In the process of rehearsing choreography, dancers constantly solve problems—making choreography work spatially, technically, and aesthetically. It is here that we synthesize and apply so much of our learning—the skill and artistry of movement, choreographic structure and design, and hearing musical meter, rhythm, tempi, pulse, and phrasing. And finally, critical thinking and analysis happen when dancers conclude whether the choreography and the way it was danced was good, and why.

Dancers also take direction and criticism, instantly process them, apply it, and present the dance sequence again. At times, a dancer takes on the role of choreographer or director and has responsibility for conducting rehearsals and giving directions to his/her peers.

Lastly, dancers are competitive as well as creative, and therefore we are resourceful and show initiative.

These attributes are the same qualities that are found in any successful career in any field or profession. But dancers don't consciously think about them; rather, they live them. Such qualities are built into their whole way of life.

SUGGESTED READING

Barringer, Janice, and Sarah Schlesinger. *The Pointe Book: Shoes, Training, and Technique*. Hightstown, N.J.: Princeton Book, 2004.

Beaumont, Cyril W. *A Manual of the Theory and Practice of Classical Theatrical Dancing (Méthode Cecchetti)*. London: C. W. Beaumont, 1922; reprint, New York: Dover, 1975.

Burrows, Terry. *How to Read Music*. New York: St. Martin's Press, 1999.

Cecchetti USA. http://www.cecchettiusa.org/enrico.htm.

Chujoy, Anatole, and P. W. Manchester, eds. *The Dance Encyclopedia*. Rev. ed. New York: Simon and Schuster, 1967.

Clarke, Mary, and Clement Crisp. *Ballerina: The Art of Women in Classical Ballet*. Pennington, N.J.: Princeton Book, 1987.

———. *Ballet Art: From the Renaissance to the Present*. New York: Clarkson N. Potter, 1978.

Cooper, Helen. *The Basic Guide to How to Read Music*. New York: Putnam, 1985.

Craske, Margaret, and Cyril W. Beaumont. *Theory and Practice of Allegro in Classical Ballet*. London: Lowe and Brydone, 1972.

Franklin, Eric. *Dance Imagery for Technique and Performance*. Champaign, Ill.: Human Kinetics, 1996.

Grant, Gail. *Technical Manual and Dictionary of Classical Ballet*. 2nd rev. ed. New York: Dover, 1967.

Grieg, Valerie. *Inside Ballet Technique: Separating Anatomical Fact from Fiction in the Ballet Class*. Pennington, N.J.: Princeton Book, 1994.

Guest, Ivor. *The Divine Virginia: A Biography of Virginia Zucchi*. New York: Marcel Deckker, 1977.

Hammond, Sandra Noll. *Ballet: Beyond the Basics*. Palo Alto: Mayfield, 1982.

———. *Ballet Basics*. 5th ed. Boston: McGraw-Hill, 2004.

Kirstein, Lincoln. *Dance: A Short History of Classic Theatrical Dancing*. Princeton, N.J.: Princeton Book, 1987.

Kostrovitskaya, Vera S. *100 Lessons in Classical Ballet*. Trans. Oleg Briansky. Garden City, N.Y.: Doubleday, 1981.

Lawson, Joan. *The Teaching of Classical Ballet: Common Faults in Young Dancers and Their Training.* 2nd ed. New York: Theatre Arts Books, 1983.

Lee, Carol. *An Introduction to Classical Ballet.* Hillsdale, N.J.: Lawrence Erlbaum Associates, 1983.

Schorer, Suki, with Russell Lee. *Suki Schorer on Balanchine Technique.* Gainesville: University Press, 2006.

Sparger, Celia. *Anatomy and Ballet.* 5th ed. New York: Theatre Arts Books, 1970.

Sweigard, Lulu E. *Human Movement Potential: Its Ideokinetic Facilitation.* New York: Dodd, Mead, 1974.

Tarasov, Nikolai Ivanovich. *Ballet Technique for the Male Dancer.* New York: Doubleday, 1985.

Vaganova, Agrippina. *Basic Principles of Classical Ballet.* Trans. Anatole Chujoy. New York: Dover, 1969.

Vincent, Lawrence M. *The Dancer's Book of Health.* Kansas City: Sheed Andrews and McMeel, 1978.

Warren, Gretchen Ward. *The Art of Teaching Ballet: Ten Twentieth-Century Masters.* Gainesville: University Press of Florida, 1999.

———. *Classical Ballet Technique.* Gainesville: University Press of Florida, 1990.

INDEX

of, 93–94, 116–18; pedagogical flexibility of, 34, 96, 105; physical toll on, 104–5; qualities and responsibilities of, 92–93, 96–97; relationships with students, 34, 91–94, 96–98, 115–18; skills required for, 99, 109; student injuries and, 125–26. *See also* teaching skills

Ballistic stretching, 67

Ballon, 114

Ballonné, 49

Ballotté, 49

Barre exercises, 40–46; connection with center floor work, 50; demonstrating, 106; *on pointe,* 50; purposes of, 36–37; sequencing, 37–40; set, 24, 34–35; tempo in, 38; time spent on, 37, 111

Barringer, Janice, 19

Bars in music, 80–81, 83

Baryshnikov, Mikhail, 14

Basic Principles of Classical Ballet: Russian Ballet Technique (Vaganova), 21, 48

Battement. See specific types

Battement passé développé, 45

Batterie, 35, 48, 50

Beat, 82, 85

Beating steps, 25

Beauchamp, Pierre, 7, 17

Beaumont, Cyril, 12–13

Bedells, Phyllis, 14

Benesh Movement Notation, 53

Blasis, Carlo, 8–10, 12, 19

Body planes, 55–57

Bournonville, August, 8, 11, 14–15

Bourrée, 19

Boys: growth spurts, 23–24, 124; men's steps, 50

Breathing, 68–69

Brisé: in *allegro,* 48, 49; *dégagé* and, 41; underlying steps for, 25

Brisé volé, 48

Bulimia, 128–29

Business plan for one's studio, 132–35

Cabriole, 48, 49, 50

Cadence, 81

Cambré, 56, 68; in barre work, 38, 39, 40

Capezio Dancewear, 73

Cartilage (meniscus), 70, 77, 124

Cecchetti, Enrico, 10, 12–13

Cecchetti Method, 1, 12–13; alternating barre sides in, 104; body position in, 26; influence of, 14; instruction in, 20, 21; points of the square, 100, *101*

Celli, Vincenzo, 1, 4

Center floor work, 46–50; *adage* in, 47; *allegro* in, 48–49; barre work as preparation for, 37; connection with barre work, 50; demonstrating, 106; movement *en diagonal,* 49; objectives for, 46; practice, 34–35, 46–47; time spent on, 37, 111; turns, 47

Center of gravity (COG), 57–58; muscle memory and, 69; raising, 60, 63, 65; visual focus and, 62

Central vertical axis, 3, 37, 56, 58, *59*, 61

Cervical curve, 64

Cervical vertebrae, 63

Chaîné, 47, 49; music for, 89, 115; spotting and, 25

Changement, 25, 48, 49

Chassé, 41

Chassé coupé, 49

Chassé coupé jeté en tournant, 49

Chest breathing, 68–69

Christiansen, Harold, 1

Chujoy, Anatole, 15

Code of Terpsichore, The (Blasis), 8–10

Collaborative skills of dancers, 137

Collagen, 122

Combinations, constructing, 35

Common time, 82–83

Compound time, 83

Rory Foster is professor emeritus of DePaul University in Chicago, where he taught for twenty-five years and held the rank of full professor and dean of the Barat Conservatory of Dance. He received his training in Chicago, New York, and London with renowned teachers from the Russian and Italian schools. He was invited to join American Ballet Theatre under the direction of Lucia Chase, where he worked with many influential choreographers including Antony Tudor, Agnes de Mille, Alvin Ailey, Peter Darrell, Eliot Feld, Birgit Cullberg, and John Neumeier. He toured throughout England, Europe, and the Far East as a principal dancer with Alexander Roy's London Ballet Theatre and later became a principal dancer with the New Orleans Ballet.

Following his performing career, Rory Foster was appointed ballet master for the New Orleans Ballet and then for the Chicago Ballet under the direction of Ruth Page and Frederic Franklin. He has been a guest teacher for many professional companies, including the Hong Kong Ballet, Cincinnati Ballet, Hubbard Street Dance Chicago, Nevada Ballet Theatre, and California Ballet. Rory also teaches extensively for university dance departments, dance festivals, and preprofessional conservatories, both nationally and internationally.